PIMLI

81

SOHO IN THE FIFTIES

Daniel Farson was born in London, the son of the American foreign correspondent Negley Farson. He travelled widely as a child and was evacuated to Canada and America during the Second World War. At the age of 17 he joined the Central Press, becoming the youngest Parliamentary and Lobby Correspondent. The following year he enlisted in the US Air Corps. He worked as a staff photographer for *Picture Post* for two years, then as a freelance journalist until he joined the Merchant Navy and sailed round the world. In 1956 he began working for Independent Television and became well known as an interviewer with series of his own such as *Farson's Guide to the British*.

In 1964 Daniel Farson turned his back on Soho and television and moved to North Devon to work as a full-time writer. His first book, *Jack the Ripper*, was a bestseller, since when he has published more than 20 books, including a biography of his great-uncle, Bram Stoker, *The Man Who Wrote Dracula*; two volumes of autobiography, *Out of Step* and *A Window on the Sea; A Traveller in Turkey; Henry: An Appreciation of Henry Williamson*; and several books combining his words and photographs: *Sacred Monsters, Escapades* and *With Gilbert and George in Moscow*. His biography of his friend Francis Bacon will be published in 1993.

SOHO IN THE FIFTIES

DANIEL FARSON

With an introduction by George Melly

PIMLICO

PIMLICO

20 Vauxhall Bridge Road, London SW1V 2SA

London Melbourne Sydney Auckland Johannesburg
and agencies throughout the world

First published by Michael Joseph Ltd 1987
Pimlico edition 1993

Typeset by Deltatype Ltd, Ellesmere Port
Printed and bound in Great Britain by

ISBN 0-7126-5724-X

For

Ian Board – and the members of
the Colony
and for
Muriel Belcher who started it

CONTENTS

Part Two: Addicted to Soho

Part Three: Resurgence for Soho

ACKNOWLEDGEMENTS

All the photographs in this book are by the author, and his copyright, with the exception of the following: Daniel Farson by John Deakin, from the author's collection; lunch at Wheeler's by John Deakin, courtesy of the Marlborough Gallery; Francis Bacon by John Deakin, from the author's collection.

The lyrics of Cole Porter, quoted on page 66 are from 'I Wish I Were in Love Again' by Richard Rodgers and Lorenz Hart, copyright 1937 Chappell & Co Inc, reproduced by permission of Chappell Music Ltd. The quotation by George Barker on page 100 is from *In Memory of David Archer* by George Barker and that by Philip Larkin on page 146 is from 'Annus Mirabilis' from *High Windows* by Philip Larkin, both reproduced by permission of Faber and Faber Ltd. The quotations by Colin MacInnes on pages 140, 146 and 148 are reproduced by permission of the Colin MacInnes Estate.

INTRODUCTION
by George Melly

This splendid book, despite its rather matter-of-fact title, is really about a love affair. It begins with a young man, fresh from Cambridge and heading, as if by instinct, towards a district which would never let him go. Today, while still strong, Farson's passion for Soho has become less obsessive, more a question of good-natured habit; he can recognise, although without bitterness, the sagging flesh and insincere mannerisms of his ageing mistress. This hasn't prevented him, however, in celebrating his salad days, from reconstructing that dreamlike decade when everything seemed possible and time alone appeared an irrelevance.

I am perhaps in as good a position as anyone to write this preface in that my experience of Soho coincides almost exactly with Dan's. Not only did I cover the same period, but I moved in the same circles, drank in the same pubs and clubs, kept the same punishing hours. I can therefore assure the reader, with complete objectivity, that this is how it was.

My own Soho, and that of many others, was intertwined with jazz and, before I write about the book itself, I would ask the reader's indulgence while I sketch its role, for this is an area of which – naturally, as it was not his particular interest – Dan makes only a passing mention. The 100 Club, then known as 'Humph's', was in Oxford Street, but it faced Soho proper and the queues on Monday and Saturday nights stretched right round the corner into north Soho or Fitzrovia, as it was known. As John Mortimer explained, 'Jazz Clubs were the temples of New Orleans and warm sex and cold coffee'. We lived for those sweaty, non-deodorised evenings, eating afterwards in a steamy little Cypriot café in New Compton Street, where the peeled potatoes in tin tubs of cold water were stored next to the lavatories.

Later on, when Humph went mainstream, his revivalist audience turned towards Cy Laurie, who had established himself in the basement of Mac's Rehearsal Rooms in Windmill Street. The first 'Alnite Rave-ups' took place there, provoking *The News of the World* into a frenzy of prurience. Then it was Ken Colyer's reign. Ken, the intransigent prophet of strict New Orleans traditionalism, preached his fundamentalist gospel from a club off Cambridge Circus.

Meanwhile the 'modernists', the early defenders of 'Bebop', had their own Soho 'scene'. There was 'Club Eleven' to start with, and that too operated from one of the studios in Mac's Rehearsal Rooms. Then, in 1958, Ronnie Scott opened his own club, first in Gerrard Street and later in Frith Street, where it still flourishes today almost thirty years later.

Almost equally long established is 'The Marquee' in Wardour Street. This started as a traditional jazz club but then, during the sixties, it became the great testing ground of emerging Rhythm and Blues groups. The Rolling Stones, for example, made their West End début there.

Throughout the fifties there were always places to jam in Soho. The subterranean Mandrake Club for example, which Dan describes in a broader context, took off most nights. There was the 'Metro', a damp basement tunnel largely patronised by rather snooty French students, and in the later fifties, the Cottage Club, strictly a fall-about station during the day, but taken over by the jazzers in the late evening. The Modern musicians also found places to improvise into the small hours although, with few exceptions, the two schools never mixed.

Nor is the story over. Dan mentions the Pizza king, Peter Boizot, in his chapters about the renaissance of Soho in recent years. He praises him for re-animating Kettner's and restoring it to its former Edwardian splendour, but he fails to remind us – perhaps he is unaware – that in the basement of Boizot's Dean Street branch, Peter nightly presents a splendidly varied jazz programme, including visiting Americans. As the basement, while packed, is small, one must presume that the music is subsidised from Boizot's Pizza Express empire.

All in all, jazz and Soho have always been compatible.

But why, the reader may ask, should Dan's rosy if bloodshot reconstruction of a time and place be of interest to those for whom the sixties, let alone the fifties, appear to be ancient history; or intrigue people, even of Farson's own generation, who were never drawn towards that dodgy never-never land, that halucinatory enclave where we waited, consumed by angst, to cure today's hangover by making certain of tomorrow's. The answer, I believe, lies partly with the skill which Dan brings to his task on a purely literary level, but partly also with the fact that within that village there roamed an exceptional collection of diverse creatures who stood at least for the right to pursue their own dreams and nightmares. The fifties were a time of austerity, of punitive conventions, of a grey uniformity which would astound even the most enthusiastic defenders of the current puritan back-lash. Soho was perhaps the only area in London where the rules didn't apply. It was a Bohemian no-go area, tolerance its password, where bad behaviour was cherished – at any rate in retrospect. Only bores were made unwelcome. Above all, as Dan recognises, despite the ferocious drinking, the promiscuity, the bitchiness, it was an *innocent* time.

The longest section of this book covers a single day and night
passed by the young Farson on his very first visit to Soho. This is
clearly a convenient device: a way of describing many places which
would have taken several weeks to discover in the ordinary course
of events, and a way of introducing a large cast of people who,
while all Soho regulars, would not in reality have surfaced so
precisely on cue. This convention works remarkably well, in that
the author uses it as a film director might, freezing a frame when he
needs to and zooming in on one of his characters to enlarge on their
previous and subsequent history. As a result, by the end of this
Ulysses-like progress we have been everywhere, met everyone,
absorbed the experience of half a lifetime within the passing of a
single twenty-four hours.

At the centre of Farson's Soho, more important even than the
French pub, than the old unreconstituted Wheeler's, than the
Caves de France or indeed anywhere else, was the Colony Room
and its proprietoress, the late Muriel Belcher. Many have tried to
explain the fascination of this imperious, foul-mouthed, witty
woman, with her strange mixture of generosity and beady financial
acumen, but Dan seems to me the first one to have caught her
totally. It is, as I know, very hard to 'sell' Muriel to people who
never knew her. You can talk of her magic, the skill she had in
fusing the diverse elements around her, of orchestrating her club so
that, night after night, a small shabby room with a bar and a few
isolated piss-artists became, by closing time, a Bacchanalia. Yet,
badly described, she can come across as no more than rude,
aggressive or even banal. Dan, however, has managed it. Only
Francis Bacon's marvellous portraits of her capture that indomitable spirit with such unsentimental respect and love. Around her
most of our best writers and painters gathered. She never leant on
them when they were poor – Bacon indeed drank there for free in
his early days, in exchange for introducing rich punters; but it
wasn't just gratitude that held them after they'd made it. She, for
her part, was as proud as a ballet mother at their success. She may
never have read a book and she knew, I suspect, very little about

art, but she could sense promise without even turning round on her famous barstool. Almost all the painters, spanning several generations, who were represented in the recent exhibition of twentieth-century British Art at the Royal Academy, were, and in many cases still are, members of the Colony Room. As Farson himself said of her at her memorial service, she 'turned life into a marvellous party'.

Muriel is only one of a whole gallery of full-length portraits which lie at the centre of this book. There's Bacon himself, of course, that most unspoilt, generous and accessible of geniuses, the tragic John Minton, disgusted with his own facility, David Archer, the gentle and impractical midwife of much of the best poetry of his time, the moody and abrasive Colin MacInnes pushing open the door of the Colony Room 'as if it had done him some injustice'. There is . . . but there's no point in my listing any further figures whether central or peripheral. They are all there, waiting between the pages of the book, ready to dance to Farson's inspired choreography.

Nevertheless there is one character of whom I feel obliged to alert you. He is the photographer, the late John Deakin, Dan's evil genius, a vicious little drunk of such inventive malice and implacable bitchiness that it's surprising he didn't choke on his own venom. And yet such was his vitality, his wit, his delighted relish in his own self-destruction, that, like Farson, we find him irresistible. It says much for Dan's skill that, without concealing or softening any aspect of Deakin's treacherous, indeed poisonous character, he persuades us to mourn his death.

Dan Farson is too honest a character to pretend that Soho is without its shadows and, in the second part of his book, these gather more often. The author himself twice tried to escape what he calls 'the district's subtle wickedness' and yet admits both times to being drawn back into 'that dangerous habit-forming escape'. In fact, his own love-hate with that small grid of streets offers the book's sub-text. Success, particularly as an early TV interviewer,

SOHO IN THE FIFTIES

offered him fame and fortune but Soho, personified by John Deakin in Dan's case, doesn't really like success. It prefers failure, and in the end there comes a time when you must fight free or go under.

Farson doesn't hesitate to show us those who were drowned by listening to the Sirens' song: Nina Hamnett, for example. Once the toast of Bohemian London and Paris, she ended her days reduced to a pathetic, incontinent old wreck, cadging her drinks and desperate to call it quits. David Archer, too, died in the poor house, unaware that lawyers were trying to trace him as he had become the heir to a legacy.

Dan, though, was of sterner stuff. He retreated, all his money gone in a glorious attempt to run a music-hall pub in the Isle of Dogs, to his parents' old house in North Devon where he became a hard-working, self-disciplined writer, pulling himself up by his own typewriter ribbon. Today his visits to Soho, while memorable, are comparatively brief, but he is no Henry V repudiating the follies of his youth. Despite some reservations, he recognises how Soho has given him much joy and many true friendships. He can handle it now and has the strength of mind to catch a taxi back to Paddington to take a train to Appledore, even if it is not always exactly the one he had intended.

If the second and shorter part of the book is darker, it too is stuffed with wonderful tragi-comic stories, and it is entirely in Dan's favour, or so I believe, that his judgements, while perceptive, are refreshingly non-judgemental. Nor is he over-nostalgic. He hails the Groucho Club, for example, as the best thing to happen for years. It is a luxurious institution which would have stood no chance in the impecunious and proudly squalid fifties.

He doesn't avoid his old haunts, however. In particular he still visits the Colony Club now run by Ian Board, Miss Belcher's ex-barman and eventual heir. Once a shy and pretty boy, Ian has become a monster of aggressive, sometimes incoherent rudeness, but Dan rightly admires his determined battle to make it *his* club, to exorcise, or at any rate keep under control, the inevitable presence of Muriel's formidable ghost.

The book concludes with a reassessment of the survivors, Francis Bacon for one and Jeff Bernard for another.* Jeff has become a celebrity and his chosen boozer, the Coach and Horses, with its notoriously abrasive landlord, Norman, is a shrine for a whole new generation of Soho fanciers. Jeff's *modus vivendi* is truly ingenious. He pays for his formidable intake of drinks by writing, very funnily, about the disastrous effect the drinks have on him.

Unlike some of his contemporaries, and despite some qualifications, Dan doesn't despair of modern Soho. In fact he identifies, and quite correctly in my view, a modest renaissance during the last few years. The suppression of most of the squalid sex-shops – an event to be praised on aesthetic rather than moral grounds, some new and first-class restaurants, the art galleries replacing peep-shows, the influx of young people determined to enjoy themselves – all these things are encouraging, and he provides a useful guide to what's going on. Elsewhere he sketches in a certain amount of history, but this is neither a guide book nor a history. It's an evocation. Ghosts, as solid as the living, walk Dan's streets. Today's survivors shed their cynicism, their sense of *déjà vu*, and grow young again. It's a remarkable achievement.

* See also postscript to this edition, p.171.

HUNTING IN SOHO

I knew little about Soho apart from the vague impression that it was a villainous spot. Like all outsiders, I was mistaken. In the fifties, Soho was blessed with innocence.

Soho has always attracted eccentrics rather than criminals. It is claimed that 'So Ho!' was the hunting cry of the Duke of Monmouth when he called to his hounds as he hunted hares – an equivalent of 'Tally-ho!' – but the name was established earlier: a fourteenth-century seal shows a hare sitting astride a hound as it blows a trumpet, with the inscription 'Sohou'. Variations of the name appear in the rate-books of St Martin's in the first half of the seventeenth century with a survey referring to 'severall tenements at a place called So Ho'. Charles II gave the land in 1677 to Monmouth his bastard son, who built a splendid house on the south side of Soho Square and used the name of 'So Ho' as a password at the battle of Sedgemoor eight years later. He was a handsome man, so beloved by his mistresses that they stitched his head back on to his body after it was severed by five clumsy chops of the executioner: they wanted him to meet his creator in one piece.

Admittedly the area near Little Pulteney Street was known as

Knave's Acre, and the hunting aspect of Soho has never ceased – though the prey is arguably more human today; but, through the ages, people have gone to Soho largely in pursuit of fun.

Casanova, the great lover, attended the first nighclubs which started in Soho. These were organised in 1760 by Térèse Cornelys at Carlisle House, which was filled with 'Chinese' and Chippendale furniture, all unpaid for. In the guise of holding a society rout-ball or masquerade, she welcomed as many as 600 'guests' to her salon at two guineas a head, but she died as penniless as the King of Corsica, who was buried in St Anne's Court on public subscription.

One of her 'regulars' was Mulin, the man who invented roller-skates and wore them when he came to call as an early form of marketing. One night he drank too much, lost his balance, skidded and crashed headlong into the expensive mirrors at the end of her room.

The Chevalier D'Eon, the most celebrated transvestite in Europe, was employed as a spy by both the French and the English (he died in London in 1810), which makes him one of the earliest and most bizarre double-agents. The French Ambassador began to fear him as a possible rival and invited him to dinner at the French Embassy in Soho Square, drugging his wine. Making his apologies, D'Eon stumbled from the room with enough presence of mind to refuse the help of two sedan carriers at the corner of the square. When he recovered, he exposed the plot after the men admitted that they had been paid to carry him in his befuddled state to the river where they had intended to throw him in. A man of almost foolhardy courage, D'Eon visited the court of Catherine the Great as himself and returned to Russia the following year as his sister.

Mozart lived at 20 Frith Street and Canaletto (who between 1746 and 1756 lived mainly in London) had his studio in 41 Beak Street, a few doors from the present offices of the *Literary Review* edited by Auberon Waugh.

Augustus Butler, described as 'a Bohemian of Bohemians', was one of the finest of the Victorian song-sheet artists. He had such a capacity for gin, referred to euphemistically as 'white satin', that he wandered around St Anne's Court during the cholera epidemic of 1885 while others fled from 'the street of the dead'. Baffled by his happy state of immunity, the doctors decided that 'he was so fortified with the spirit of his choice that he was rendered cholera-proof'.

In the early nineteenth century De Quincey, the 'opium-eater', roamed the streets searching for his Ann, the girl he fell in love with on sight and could never find again. Hazlitt lived at 6 Frith Street; his house is now restored as a small hotel.

It is ironic that Karl Marx and Logie Baird lived in Soho, for politics and last night's television are rarely discussed in Soho, though they are the mainstay of conversation in most British pubs.

One of the most colourful residents was fictitious: R. L. Stevenson's murderous Mr Hyde.

Soho has always been a state of mind rather than a boundary, adapting to those who came here from abroad, anxious to start a new life in a new home: Greeks who escaped from the Turks in the 1670s, and gave their name to Greek Street; families who left France after the Revolution, following the Huguenots who had fled to England after the revocation of the Edict of Nantes in 1685; Italians; Cypriots; Chinese; and more recently Vietnamese – all have contributed their skills and tastes. Refusing to accept the ghetto role of strangers in a strange land, they became an integral part of Soho, adding to its flavour.

Where is Soho? Its frontiers have never been clearly defined, but in 1951 it stretched north of Oxford Street with a score of public houses used by poets and painters, and classic restaurants like L'Etoile in Charlotte Street, founded by Madame Rossi at the turn of this century. Today, Soho has shifted southwards, incorporating the new Chinatown of Gerrard Street. You could say that it is bound loosely within the four circuses of Piccadilly, Oxford, Cambridge and St Giles. But the heart of Soho lay then, as it does now, between the four parallels of Wardour Street, Dean Street, Frith Street and Greek Street.

PART ONE
SOHO LIFE IN A DAY

9.00 a.m. Places and People

To the young especially, Soho is irrestible, for it offers a sort of freedom. When I arrived there in 1951, London was suffering from post-war depression and it was a revelation to discover people who behaved outrageously without a twinge of guilt and drank so recklessly that when they met the next morning they had to ask if they needed to apologise for the day before.

For a few hours in the morning when the outsiders had vanished, Soho reverted to village life with the residents greeting each other in their native tongue while their children were at school, chattering away in their new, communal language of English. Tarts, petty crooks and simple Soho people collected their milk from the two gentle old ladies who ran the Welsh dairy at the bottom of Frith Street; the French bought their croissants from Madame Valerie's; the Italian barber gave his first 'Tony Curtis' of the day; and the bookseller wrapped his first sale in plain brown paper – for there were 'dirty bookshops' even then.

Across the four parallel streets lay numerous alleys like the branches of an old tree, with Old Compton Street at the base leading into Brewer Street, lined with restaurants and food and wine stores, such as Randall & Aubin where Roma Galer looked after the till, and the Lina Stores two doors away with freshly made pasta and bags of risotto rice.

Blocks of ice left outside the shuttered restaurants started to dribble across the pavements, and kept the fish fresh at Richards (opposite the Lina), noted for such rare delicacies as Mediterranean squid and sardines.

The markets started to bustle: Rupert Street market running down to Shaftesbury Avenue was the posher of the two, with the noisier and cheaper Berwick Street market heading north.

I waited in an unpretentious café at the corner of Dean Street and Old Compton Street called Torino's, which had been run for fourteen years by Mr and Mrs Minella from Italy and their son. It was pleasantly old-fashioned with tall, arched windows, and opened at eight-thirty in the morning, closing at seven o'clock in the evening.

It had wrought-iron tables with marble tops, cups of proper coffee, and vol au vents at one shilling and sixpence. Officially it was a restaurant serving pizza, spaghetti and risotto, but you could talk for hours over a small cup of coffee and the Minellas did not mind. They were so anxious to keep their customers happy that they kept their prices low and were rash enough to allow credit. They even let me buy pâté down the street and eat it with a simple order of brown toast. Their goodwill was reciprocated and the tables were usually crowded. There were dark Italians huddled in earnest discussion, suddenly bursting into furious argument; a large woman opposite me with a Pomeranian who had painted toenails (the dog, I mean); and several pale young artists and poets searching half-heartedly for jobs.

I was about to start one myself, as a photographer for *Picture Post*. I had left Cambridge University several months earlier, where I had been paid for by the generous GI Bill of Rights, for I had enlisted in the American Army Air Corps. Before that I had been the youngest Parliamentary correspondent at the age of seventeen, for an ancient press agency where no one else was young enough to be mobile; and before that I had seen much of the world travelling in the wake of my father, the American foreign correspondent, Negley Farson. Yet few people were less worldly than I was at the age of twenty-four. My naïvety was almost obscene, but as soon as I stepped into Soho I felt that I belonged.

As I waited in Torino's, my belief that something wonderful might happen was echoed throughout Soho for, as I came to realise, this was a land of anticipation, if seldom realised. Groups gathered expectantly at street corners, though it was hard to tell their purpose. Musicians met outside their union in Archer Street hoping for employment, many armed with violin cases like gangsters gathering for a Valentine's Day massacre. A queue of expressionless men formed outside the Windmill Theatre with the promise of seeing naked girls in static poses, while muscular men pranced around Mike Solomon's gym with the dream of becoming the next contender. Optimists lounged around the bookies' runners in Frith Street, hoping for their horse to come in. Strangers like myself paused and were caught in the web, trapped as if in the buffet of some monstrous station, destined to miss our train.

A man who wore dark glasses tried the door of the York Minster in Dean Street and waited outside; and, lifting his face to catch the sun, missed the beautiful girl who walked past him barefoot. At 11.30 a.m., later than the other pubs, the bolts were drawn back and the doors of the York Minster opened – the loveliest moment of the day. The man in dark glasses went inside and I followed.

'Good morning,' said the barmaid.

'Christ, I feel awful,' said the man, and downed his first drink with a shudder. 'Ah, that feels better!'

Gaston and the French

Dean Street became the pivot of Soho for me, starting with the York Minster opposite St Anne's Church as my first real port of call. This had been ecclesiastical property and the name of the York Minster was chosen by the old wine shop as a befitting compliment. Conversely, the spire of St Anne's sports a large barrel, reconstructed today.

The inapposite name has led to confusion. One day a clergyman ordered a drink and told Gaston, the proprietor, 'I'm from the York Minster.'

'You're *in* the York Minster!'

'The other York Minster. We've received some of your goods: a dozen cases of wine, we were so pleased until we realised there was some mistake.' The labels had been addressed correctly but folded so that only 'Dean' was visible, but not 'Street', so the shipment was delivered to the Dean at the Cathedral, to his delight – until the mystery was explained.

Gaston's parents came to England in 1900, living in a room near Covent Garden which was so tiny that Madame Berlemont had to move their bed in order to open the door wide enough to admit her husband's bicycle when he came home from work. Victor Berlemont had come to learn English, though he never succeeded, serving in a number of restaurants until he became headwaiter at the European at 48 Dean Street. This was next to the Wine House – as the York Minster was known at the start of the century – which was owned by a German, Herr Schmidt. When the owner of the European died in 1910, the Berlemonts bought it from his widow and Victor cooked while his wife served. It would have been difficult to have eaten more than two shillings' worth, judging by the enormous choice on the menu for 19 August 1912, which included lobster mayonnaise for ten pence and rumpsteak frite sixpence. In 1913, before the outbreak of war, Herr Schmidt was deported and rumour has it – though Gaston denies it – that his mother ran around Soho borrowing money and bought the York Minster for £50. He was born there the following year – 'upstairs'.

Victor Berlemont, the only foreigner to have an English pub licence, was a kindly man with a white handlebar moustache, whose portrait smiles benevolently among the signed photographs of French celebrities which decorate the walls, including Maurice Chevalier and Carpentier the boxer who scribbled, 'I went to

Berlemonts' in whose cellar a ring was fixed up for my use.' In the Second World War, Berlemonts' became an obvious rendezvous for the French Resistance, and was patronised by General de Gaulle. Gaston has maintained his father's tradition, sporting the same luxuriant moustaches, and handing out red, white and blue rosettes on the Quatorze Juillet – Bastille Day. Inevitably, the pub became known as 'the French'.

Gaston is a genius of a landlord, either welcoming guests with a cheerfulness which warms the day, or throwing one out with such courtesy that one thanks him for doing so. He has lent money without losing friendship, and he dismisses drunks with diplomatic finesse: 'One of the two of us will have to go, and I'm afraid it's not going to be me!'

'Good evening, Madame,' I heard him say fulsomely one evening, followed by a 'Pardon, I mean Monsieur' – this addressed to a small, painted youth who was driven out by Gaston's quizzical stare.

He is far too shrewd to be saintly and would not have lasted so well otherwise. He has a Gallic single-mindedness and refuses to serve draught beer, making a greater profit from Pernod and wine which he imports himself. As a boy, before he went to St Anne's School up the street, he helped his father bottle wine – 'I managed twenty-four dozen bottles of wine in two hours.' At that time a Medoc cost one shilling and ninepence and a twelve-year-old port four shillings and sixpence. Gaston opens when he chooses, usually closing on Saturday night; though I have noticed that while other pubs put up their shutters when the football fans invade London, he stays open and they behave impeccably. He has seldom known trouble; it was the Admiral Duncan which suffered from the race gangs in the thirties, when a young policeman was thrown through a window and half his face was paralysed.

But there have been moments. A gang attacked the stage door of a theatre one evening and killed the commissionaire, bursting into the French shortly after it opened.

'Give me four fucking pints,' one of the men demanded.

Gaston noticed that he had blood on his sleeve. 'Ah! Get away,' he replied, 'buzz off.'

'Wot!' exclaimed the bruiser, 'you won't serve me?'

'No,' said Gaston, 'hop it.'

The man turned to his friends, described by Gaston as 'three of the biggest flat-nosed, cauliflower-eared crooks' he had ever seen.

'Give us *eight* fucking pints,' yelled the biggest.

By now Gaston was feeling frantically behind him for the emergency button. He found it and jumped over the counter, where he was joined by his father, the chef with a carving knife and two taxi-drivers who had wandered in from the rank. After a pantomime skirmish, the villains ran out of the pub. At that time an ancient cannon served as a post for horses at the corner of Church Street, now Romilly Stret, a few doors away, and by chance a drunk in a top-hat had paused there for a moment to regain his balance and gazed with astonishment at the men tumbling towards him chased by Gaston and the chef with the carving knife.

'What are you looking at?' shouted the first bruiser – 'wham!'

The same thing happened with the second and third members of the gang, leaving the old man on his knees. The fourth villain ran straight into a taxi. The police arrived a few minutes later but by then the pub was back to normal.

'Trouble?' muttered Gaston. 'No trouble here. *What* old fellow outside?'

They called the next day to tell him that the fourth man was charging Gaston with breaking some ribs.

'Don't worry,' said the policeman, 'we're charging *him* with murder.'

Gaston has always favoured the ladies with his special attention, kissing their hands as he peers lasciviously into their eyes, remembering their faces from earlier visits as he makes them feel particularly welcome. In the fifties when I arrived, he was equally courteous to the ladies off the street, for this was before the Wolfenden Report tidied up the tarts. Far from importuning, they regarded the French as a sanctuary and complained indignantly to Gaston if any man dared to pick them up, even though they had been 'on the game' a few minutes earlier. Once inside the French they were off-duty and behaved with the hauteur of hostesses before they returned to the street-corner with a clip-clop of platform shoes under dyed hair and rabbit fur, and the persuasive chirrup of 'Hullo dearie!' from a doorway.

The tarts have vanished, barmaids and barmen have come and gone, but the French has never lost its atmosphere. Wisely, Gaston has resisted attempts to do it up, though it cannot be described as a comfortable pub for it is hard to sit down when the room – for that is all it is – becomes crowded. It is not a 'sitting-down' sort of place; and this is one of the significant differences between Soho and St Germain where artists sat at the tables of the Café Flore or Les Deux Magots, over cups of coffee or *citron pressé*. In Soho you go to Madame Valerie's for your morning coffee but you go to 'the French' to *drink*. There is no distraction from this objective, no hellish fruit machine, no jukebox to interrupt. Of all the pubs, the French is the truest to the spirit of Soho. And of all the landlords, Gaston has the most panache. Once Eva, a lovely but difficult woman, became so exasperated by the boredom of listening to one of his more tiresome regulars that she threw her glass of wine in the man's face. During the appalled silence which followed, Gaston came round the bar and the customers waited for him to ban her for ever.

'Madame,' he smiled, eyeing her up and down in his quizzical way, 'I see that your glass is empty. Please allow me to refill it for you.' That is Soho style.

A Soho Type of Person
The drinkers in the French symbolised Soho in 1951.

What makes a Soho type of person? You need a Bohemian streak to find the lure irresistible. You would never contemplate going out for 'just the one' unless it was the one *day*. Soho people rarely use 'drink' in the singular – 'let's meet for a drink' or 'we'll discuss it over a drink' – for they know that such singularity is absurd. Yet they take offence if someone asks them if they want 'another' for the semblance of self-discipline is vital.

An alcoholic hates drink; the Soho person loves it. This is why there are so few alcoholics in Soho though plenty of drunks.

Soho people do not tell 'jokes' and avoid the eyes of those who do. They relish true stories, especially of their friends' disasters. Equally they enjoy celebrating a friend's success . . . when the friend is paying. The good luck might rub off.

A Soho person is someone:

who is not afraid to cry in public;
who rarely travels by public transport, preferring the privacy of taxis;
who regards taxes of the other sort, and all brown envelopes with little windows, as an unwarrantable intrusion;
who cashes cheques anywhere, except the bank;
who seldom knows the date;
who will miss a dinner appointment if he is enjoying himself;
who has been barred from at least one pub, club or restaurant;
whose life staggers from the gutter to the Ritz and maybe back again.

12.00 noon Still at the French

As the drinkers started to congregate in the French after midday, sidling inside until the first drink restored their confidence, I observed them from my corner-table and grew to know them over the following weeks: the smartly dressed elderly man whose aim in life was to leave his family and settle in a small village in Spain by himself – a common fantasy rarely fulfilled but fun to contemplate;

a man with a false Riviera suntan just out of prison; a girl in a tight black sweater sipping Pernod on her own, her face mask-white, her eyes heavily blackened around the edges, her lips bloodless and her long hair orange, who told me that she came to Soho as 'a refuge from my family and myself'.

The pub dog was known as Peter Mons Berlemont, 'Mons' being short for Monsieur. He was a disgruntled terrier, who snapped at the ankles of customers he disliked and barked angrily at the street-singer when she screamed outside, refusing to let her in. He adored the artist Nina Hamnett and sat beside her protectively at the table next to mine: 'You couldn't buy me a drink could you love, hah!'

A young man with a pudding-basin haircut was a lamplighter who started work at 4.30 p.m. The nondescript man was a film-director: the unkempt, smiling woman with tragic eyes and an old woolly coat was buying drinks for her friends because she had just been given the sack – and that is very Soho: few Soho people would celebrate if they found a job.

A one-armed accordionist, the street-singer's hated rival, played Neapolitan melodies in the sunlight outside; brown as a berry and wearing a beret, he commuted from Croydon.

An old gentleman with a startling resemblance to Edward VII, complete with cigar, spoke in French; and I was startled to hear an obvious tart say to another, 'It's my birthday tomorrow, my seventieth.' I looked at her with new respect.

'Soho is death,' said the man still wearing his dark glasses. 'I spend so much money buying drinks for other people, people I don't even *like*!' He returned time and again because he was lonely and he was lonely even though he had three wives and had just married again.

Madame Valerie, who ran the Patisserie in Old Compton Street, had her regular corner-seat. Phyllis, a cockney, eighty years old and always wearing the same hat, sat interminably over a Reids Stout and gave sudden, piercing whistles through the gap in her teeth.

'Young man, I remember London when there wasn't a single picture palace. I don't like life any more, no I don't, people aren't the same.'

The age-old complaint, and the complaint of old-age. Yet she seemed to enjoy herself in the French.

Benjamin the onion-seller called after his morning tour of the restaurants where he sold 20 strings of onions at six shillings each, earning as much as £25 a month with all expenses paid. Before the war 130 onion-sellers came each year, staying for 6 months, but now there were only 40.

Benjamin complained that most of the French had gone from Soho: 'Now too many Jews and Greeks, I don't know where they come from.' (Israel and Greece, perhaps?) 'It's very bad for business. These Cypriots, they prefer to buy trash on the market.'

He was proud of his onions, large and firm, and while he talked a woman nipped one off the string on his back and took it home for her dinner. He realised but did not mind.

One man in particular caught my attention. It would have been surprising if he had not, for his appearance was arresting when he entered the French earlier with the gait of a midget wrestler and stood beside me so that I was able to observe him closely. I noticed that he looked curiously dishevelled, as if he had just been rescued at sea and fitted out in clothes donated by the crew. These consisted of paint-smeared blue jeans, whose flies were open, and a thick white polo-neck sweater, now grey with age, on to which spots of blood had fallen earlier from the ridge of congealed gore behind his ear. Over this ensemble, he wore a British officer's 'warm', a graveyard for cigarette burns and wine stains, which he clasped to himself like a mandarin. As if he knew that I was watching him, he suddenly turned round with a hideously forced grimace, revealing a jagged row of discoloured teeth which he clenched so noisily that I could hear them snap. His flirtatious eyes were bloodshot, his cheeks pockmarked, and a glimpse inside his mouth disclosed a tongue the colour of aubergine.

Fascinated by such presence, I listened as Gaston greeted him:

'Good morning, Mr Deakin. I hope you don't feel as bad as you look?'

The man, now identified as 'Mr Deakin', shook his head grimly: 'Far worse. What would be good for me?'

'Well, you should know!' Gaston exclaimed. 'May I suggest a Fernet-Branca, perhaps?'

'Anything. I swallowed a raw egg in a glass of milk earlier but it was halfway down before I realised it was bad.'

Gaston shuddered: 'I gather you had quite a night?'

'Did I leave my camera here?'

'You might have given it to someone else but not to me. That will be three shillings and sixpence.'

'For this muck! You must be joking, Gaston.' He searched through his pockets in vain, opening and shutting his mouth several times like a ventriloquist's dummy. 'I'll have to settle later.'

At this moment he was saved by the arrival of a distinguished man who might have been a judge or a bank manager.

'Oh, there you are,' said Mr Deakin ungraciously, 'you're just in time to pay for this, and can you lend me a pound while you're about it?'

'Dear me, I gave you a pound yesterday.'

'Well, I need another today.'

The distinguished man reluctantly produced a pound but far from receiving thanks he was told to 'shove off' instead.

'Bejesus,' said Mr Deakin, 'how you bore me,' ordering himself a large pink gin with the note he had just been given.

The stranger shot me an embarrassed, lop-sided smile: 'I do apologise for my friend,' he said, giving me a slight bow, and the bank-manager image went quickly out of focus as he raised his voice and gave a slight stamp of his feet. 'He's such a *silly* little man! Ah, well . . .' After standing there with obvious irritation he made as dignified an exit as possible.

Deakin recognised another friend at the other end of the bar and left abruptly.

As the French filled up, he was now the centre of a lively group regaling them with some adventure. The dandruff on his shoulders was spotlit by the rays of cruel sunlight which filtered through the windows, picking out individual customers as if they were actors on a stage.

He was talking to a stylish couple: a handsome man who wore dark glasses (though not the man I had seen earlier), and a high-necked dark-blue sweater under a well-cut suit; she wore a cream-coloured jacket over a dark-grey dress and fussed at her cigarette with an arrogance which suited her upturned nose.

She pitched her voice as if she wanted people to overhear: 'The food at the Caprice last night,' she exclaimed, raising her eyes, 'well, really!' she giggled. 'Aren't I right, Michael?' she demanded, kicking his shin.

'Of course you are,' he agreed hastily.

'And the Milroy afterwards,' she continued, 'have you ever known anything so *boring*! All those people!' They laughed incredulously.

She might have wanted her remarks to be overheard but she swung round aggressively when she noticed me hovering. 'And what do *you* want?'

'I met Mr Deakin earlier,' I apologised, 'though I'm not sure if he remembers me.' This was not strictly true for we had scarcely exchanged a word, but it served as an introduction.

'That's simply amazing!' She tossed back her head and shook it delightedly like a dog emerging from the water. 'He never remembers anyone . . . and *Mister* Deakin!'

'Would you like a drink?' I asked.

'Would I! I was hoping someone would ask. This lot – really!'

Deakin introduced himself as 'John' – though I continued to think of him as 'Deakin' – and then his companions with an absurd flourish: 'May I have the honour of presenting Michael and Henrietta Law.'

Michael was to become a close friend and I thought that Henrietta was the most attractive woman I had ever seen.

Henrietta was not her real name (that was something like Margery) but Michael changed the names of all his wives if he thought he could choose one more suitable, as he usually did. In his autobiography (*Not All a Ball*), John Moynihan described her as 'the Lady Brett of Soho'; and though they may have had little else in common she too could stop people in their tracks and make them turn round, at first shocked by her caustic wit, and then lost in admiration.

Deakin accepted the offer of a drink with a gentility which did not suit him – 'That's awfully kind of you', – and she mocked him accordingly – 'Orfully kind of you, wot'; though this did not deter him from asking for a *large* pink gin. Michael took the drink distractedly, looking at his watch as if he were late for an appointment and this was an imposition, but he accepted it nevertheless.

Then his face brightened: 'Henrietta, look! Nigel.'

She clapped her hands delightedly, jumping up and down like the little girl she tried so hard to be, and left without a word of thanks.

'Have you no pride?' Deakin called after them.

She turned round briefly: '*None.*'

'Their meal ticket's just walked in,' Deakin explained. 'He's as rich as Croesus and he takes them everywhere to keep him company – dinner at the Caprice before they go on to the Milroy and so on; but he never buys them what they *need*, like the taxi fare home, so they have to walk all the way back from the Milroy. No wonder they're sick of it.'

I laughed, for he spoke so seriously, and he looked at me with new interest.

'Do you know what he did yesterday? Nigel said he was going upstairs to eat and would they like to join him?' (At this time there was an excellent restaurant on the first floor, serving that rarity: good, simple French food, perfectly cooked and without pretension. It became a favourite place and I lunched there once with Ken Tynan and Patrick Campbell; they were both celebrated stutterers, and I felt that I had been through a car-wash by the end of the meal.) 'Well, halfway up the stairs, he turned round and asked them if they had any money. Of course they hadn't' – Deakin lowered his voice to a deafening stage-whisper – 'so he told them: "If you like, you can come up and watch me eat." Have you ever heard of anything so mean?'

'I think it's rather funny.'

'I don't know why he wanted those bums in the first place, but he wasn't joking. They didn't get a bite, just a glass of his wine . . .'

He broke off as Henrietta hurried over, looked at me suspiciously and hugged Deakin passionately. 'Nigel's invited us to lunch,' she told him breathlessly. 'This time he really means it and we're starving, so you won't mind.' She waved to us as they went upstairs.

Deakin looked around him warily and offered me a drink in a conspiratorial voice as if it was illegal. I did not realise what a special occasion this was, though I noticed that he counted his coins on the counter as if they were foreign currency.

'*Uno* gin, *per favore*.'

'Yes, Mr Deakin,' the French barman sighed.

'Ciao *caro*, and something for the child.'

'Good heavens, John,' said a voice behind us. 'It's so long ago since you last bought a drink that I'm surprised you don't use sovereigns.'

I turned to see Deakin's distinguished friend, standing there with a clutch of books under one arm and his seedy raincoat over the other. He laughed loudly when he recognised me and gave me a sort of bow. His laugh lasted too long and died of its own accord.

'Shove off,' said Deakin, with surprising cruelty.

'Oh dear me,' said his friend. He looked undecided for a moment, then he went.

Deakin faced me with guilty, spaniel eyes: 'He's rather special.'

That was my introduction to John Deakin, one of the finest photographers of the century, and to David Archer, the bookseller and publisher of poets.

John Deakin

At that time John Deakin worked for *Vogue*, where he had the perfect set-up. The offices were conveniently close to the French, around the corner in Shaftesbury Avenue where Deakin's back-cloth was available and quickly lit by such talented assistants as Tom Hawkyard. When there was a photo-call, Deakin would make his appearance, take several full-face and profile shots, and hurry back to Gaston. There was no time for the niceties of cheese.

On learning that I was a photographer too, he was flattered by the prospect of an admiring fan and invited me to the Bayswater flat which he shared with David Archer. When he showed me his prints I was stunned by their excitement. I have no illusions about the 'art' of photography, knowing how much a photographer depends on his darkroom and an imaginative lay-out editor who can transform an indifferent, even a blurred photo into a masterpiece; and there is no denying Deakin's good fortune in having the *Vogue* darkroom staff to back him up with their immense prints giving the harsh contrast he demanded. But the eye was Deakin's. As he presented the prints for my inspection, laying them out on the floor with the wistful anxiety of a haberdasher showing his cloth, I was genuinely shocked by their impact. They were frequently portraits to recoil from, with the stark reality of prison mug-shots. Every spot was magnified, every pore exposed, dandruff resembling a fall of snow, an unshaven chin a forest. Cecil Beaton's portraits were insipid by comparison.

Deakin's sitters became his victims and I was startled to learn, when I read an extract from *Eight Portraits* (an unpublished typescript now belonging to Bruce Bernard), that he thought of them in this way too:

Being fatally drawn to the human race, what I want to do when I photograph it is to make a revelation about it. So my sitters turn into my victims. But I would like to add that it is only those with a demon, however small and of whatever kind, whose faces lend themselves to be

victimised at all. And the only complaints I have had from my victims
have been from the bad ones, the vainies, the meanies.

Even so, I suspect that Mother Theresa would have emerged as
a nervous meanie by the time Deakin was through with her.

Deakin's 'victims' were largely Soho people: Dylan Thomas in
the graveyard at Laugharne, waist-deep in weeds; George Barker
posing vainly in a public lavatory; John Davenport; David Archer.

Deakin's relationship with Archer was an odd one. What made
it even odder was Deakin's candour, for if his photographs were
shocking, his life was outrageous – I had never heard such
disclosures before.

John Deakin was born near the leper colony in Bootle on 5 May
1912. His family left Liverpool soon afterwards and moved to
Cheshire, where his father worked as a warehouse supervisor for
Lever Brothers in the Wirral. When he was eighteen, Deakin went
to Dublin, where he became involved with 'theatricals' in some
capacity never fully explained, and in due course he moved to
London where he was arrested in a homosexual nightclub. Though
this was only his second night in London, Deakin had acquired a
'benefactor' who paid for a young and up-and-coming barrister to
defend him, which he did successfully, though it was Deakin
himself who caused the proverbial 'sensation in court' when the
prosecuting counsel asked him if he found it odd that members of
the same sex should dance together:

'Why should I?' Deakin protested indignantly. 'I had just
arrived in this country. How should I know what you do? It seems
to me the English do all sorts of curious things.' He wanted to add,
'After all, you are wearing a perfectly frightful wig!'

The fact that Deakin was English himself was overlooked, for he
had the only barrister and his was the only acquittal.

Soon he was living with the American millionaire and art-
collector, Arthur Jeffress. One afternoon they went to a neighbour's house for tea on the Wiltshire lawn where there were several
guests whose names were mumbled in the introduction.

When a frisky dachshund started running around in circles, one of the women called out sharply, 'Deakin, Deakin, come here.'

'That's an odd name,' said Jeffress slyly.

'Yes, isn't it,' she laughed. 'It's quite an amusing story actually. Of course he's frightfully successful now,' she gave a nod towards her husband who had risen to a junior post in the government, such as assistant to the Attorney General, 'but you wouldn't believe what a struggle he had when he started. We named this little monster Deakin because it was the name of the first person he defended in the first case he won when he became a barrister. Darling, do tell them,' she called across to her husband. 'I'm sure we're all broad-minded and it's really terribly funny. It was one of those pansy cases.'

'Well, it was funny,' her husband agreed, 'but perhaps I shouldn't?'

'Oh do,' everyone chorused, including Jeffress, but at that moment the junior minister caught sight of Deakin (the man, not the dog) and their eyes met in shocked recognition. 'No,' said the shaken junior minister, 'anyhow, it's time that we were going.'

Now Deakin lived with David Archer and I found that the most baffling relationship of all, for Archer paid the entire rent for the spacious apartment. I was bemused by Deakin's casual reference to Archer's 'favourite whip'. Deakin had no compunction in telling me that he had shouted at Archer the previous night while Archer fumbled for something in a chest of drawers. 'What are you doing?'

'I'm looking for my favourite whip,' Archer explained.

'Oh, for God's sake!'

'You're not supposed to shout at me,' Archer protested. 'I'm supposed to shout at you.' When Archer came fussing into the apartment a few moments later, I gazed at this distinguished man with astonishment.

David Archer

Archer had a good face. It revealed all the strengths of the man and none of his weaknesses, until the respectable façade was shattered as he suddenly raised his voice and stamped his feet. He was the kindest of all the 'characters' I met in Soho. My first impression was that of a soberly dressed man with grey hair and spectacles who stood erect. He looked so conventional that he might have been a distinguished judge, or a grand butler on his day off. When he had a tantrum and the façade exploded, the resemblance was closer to a neurotic Nazi. Though usually the mildest of men with impeccable manners, he had the knack of causing unusual scenes.

His background was grand: he had a stately home in Wiltshire and a father who was a military man confined to a wheelchair. Archer borrowed my bowler hat when he went to Major Archer's funeral and left it on the train on the way back. His father's death left a mother who doted on her son and worried ceaselessly.

When Archer started taking daily dips in the Serpentine, she managed to contact Deakin by telephone: 'I am most concerned about David. One day I feel that he'll swim and swim and swim . . .'

'That's all right, Mrs Archer,' said Deakin, 'as it's the Serpentine he'll just come out the other side.'

Archer was due to inherit but this blessing proved his curse, for he had succumbed to the plausibility of money-lenders and was pecking away at his inheritance like a voracious hen. The money he spent was always for the benefit of others, for though he may have enjoyed his ability to be generous it did not diminish his generosity.

Archer had a lame right arm which he concealed by clutching books or magazines. I doubt if anyone would have noticed it, but it worried Archer a great deal and exempted him from military service, which is a shame for he would have relished that peculiar hierarchy. Instead, he devoted his energies to social work in the war and ran a youth club in Glasgow which had to fold after the boys stole everything there was to steal, down to the last stick of furniture.

All this made Archer endearing; his skill as a publisher made him exceptional. He possessed an astounding nose for talent, though how he developed this gift is mysterious, for he liked the *idea* of writers and their books rather than the books themselves. He read by instinct, usually half a book rather than a whole one, and took a special interest in the covers; and if he went to the theatre he *invariably* left in the interval. When Deakin took him to the ballet he told me that Archer started to complain loudly in the dress circle.

'What are they supposed to be doing now?'

'Shush, be quiet, David. This is *Swan Lake* and those are cygnets.'

'They don't look like bloody cygnets to me, I'm buzzing off.'

Yet he was so perceptive that he published the best poets of his time *before* they were famous. With the editor of the *Sunday Referee* he printed *18 Poems* by Dylan Thomas when the poet was only eighteen in 1934. It sold then at three shillings and sixpence a copy but today would fetch several hundred pounds. I was told a legendary story that Archer held a party to celebrate the publication of the poems and when they met the following day he asked Dylan if he had enjoyed it.

'I hear it was a very good party,' Dylan Thomas replied stiffly, 'but you forgot to invite me.'

'Oh, silly me,' said Archer.

This sounded unlikely until I knew Archer.

When I narrated *A Gentleman of Soho* (on 4 February 1975), an affectionate tribute to Archer produced for BBC Radio by Maurice Leitch, I discovered that Archer's achievements were more substantial than I had realised. In the early 1930s, around the time that Deakin found himself in court, Archer ran a bookshop in Parton Street which became a refuge for young writers, and he encouraged them in the most practical way possible by publishing their work under the imprint of the Parton Press, allowing them to retain the copyright.

George Barker went to the bookshop one morning in the spring of 1931 or 1932, when he heard that there was an eccentric gentleman interested in publishing books of verse.

The bookshop was full of bright marvellous books – lovely colours – the whole place looked charming – rather like spring flowers; and in these spring flowers stood this figure who I took to be a character lost out of both Wodehouse and Proust at the same time. If I remember rightly, he was dressed in a rather elegant Jermyn Street grey suit – he was in fact mending the shop – that is, he'd got up a ladder, turned to me as I entered the bookshop and said: 'Be an angel – hand me that hammer', and that was the first sentence David uttered to me and I handed him the hammer though he seemed likely to bang his finger or something like that – he was incapable of banging a nail in.

They went across the road to a café called Megs and six months later Archer suggested that he might publish a book of Barker's verse, which he did under the title *Preliminary Poems*.

I don't think he had any Christian ideas at all, but in practice he was something very like a secular saint . . . his concern with other people was the most moral thing about him. He got into tantrums if he didn't get his own way but I think in the centre of the man's nature there was the most profound love and concern and passion for other people. That was what I found most deeply moving about him – his love for other human beings.

Philip Toynbee, who had run away from school, remembered the bookshop in 1934 as the prototype of all the left-wing bookshops and people's libraries which came later, with Soviet posters on the walls and the bright yellow jackets of Gollancz's Left Book Club.

Archer himself seemed the perfect figure to preside in a place of this kind. The atmosphere at the shop was deeply and splendidly conspiratorial. Looking back on the few days I spent in Parton Street I have a vision of cloaked and daggered figures hastily looking up and down the street before slipping surreptitiously inside. I'm not sure whether Archer was himself a member of the Communist party either then or afterwards, for neither he nor Esmond [Romilly] nor the general atmosphere of the shop was really Communist in the Party sense of the word. Archer was possessed by a passionate love of all that was newest and freshest in the literature of that time, and it was this strongly literary overtone which distinguished the Parton Street shop from those of the many successors whose chief object was not to sell poetry but to provide ammunition for the class struggle.

Never afraid to declare his feelings, Archer raced out of the shop one evening when he saw John Strachey go by, then at the peak of his extreme left-wing United Front phase. He was due to speak at a rally in Conway Hall and as Archer buttonholed him fiercely Maurice Richardson looked on: 'I couldn't hear what he said, but Strachey backed away in alarm.'

'I was telling him to pitch it hot and strong,' said Archer when he came back into the shop, 'but he seemed to think I was an *agent provocateur*. If only he wouldn't groan like a constipated curate.'

His allegiance was absolute. Once he kicked a critic who gave a bad review to a friend.

'David, you can't go around kicking critics, it isn't done,' someone protested.

Archer hummed and hawed as was his wont. 'Well, one does get rather fussed,' he explained. 'Anyhow, it was only a *tiny* kick.'

The Parton Bookshop was doomed. Preferring 'a cosy chat' with his poets at Megs or the nearest pub, he resented the demands of running a business. Publishers' bills were unpaid, so he had to go round personally with the cash in hand to collect a book that someone ordered, and his credit was cut off. The shop was taken over in 1936. I believe that Archer felt guilty at receiving a family allowance rather than earning it through hard work, or even winning it on a horse race which could be seen as a glorious stroke of luck to be shared happily. He excelled in the grace of giving, sometimes going to absurd lengths in order to save a friend's embarrassment as he put a pound note, or two, in an empty matchbox and slipped it into someone's pocket – a rash procedure, for sometimes the boxes were thrown away by mistake.

Though he described Archer as 'a dicey Duchess', the poet Paul Potts remembered his generosity when it was less furtive:

Once I gave a lecture for him in Glasgow and he paid me the fee in the
way a young subaltern in the Guards would have opened a
carriage for an old lady seventy-five years ago. The actual physical way
in which he gave money was the most beautiful thing about him. It was
as if he was conferring the OM on you, and all the honour was to you
and not to him. He really believed his function in life was to look after
people who couldn't look after themselves, provided they had some
talent.

What his family made of him, I cannot imagine. Elizabeth
Smart said that they never really understood him, and she
suspected that Major Archer believed that his son was filling
chorus girls' slippers with champagne. Shortly after I met him,
Archer invited Deakin down to the family home in Wiltshire, and
as I doubted if Deakin was parental material (a doubt I confirmed
later to my cost) when I met him in Soho afterwards I asked Archer
how the visit had gone.

'Oh, the silly man!' he exclaimed. 'He got drunk, of course, and
never turned up, and cook had gone to a great deal of trouble. After
all' – and here he let out a loud discomfited sigh – 'he was the first
guest I'd invited down for twenty-nine years.'

Perhaps Deakin provided a necessary friction, for he and Archer
remained friends after they were asked to leave the spacious
apartment in Bayswater and Deakin moved into a small top flat of
his own in Berwick Street, within easy staggering distance of Dean
Street.

Deakin must have received a reasonable salary from *Vogue* yet
constructed his façade of abject poverty so convincingly that it
never occurred to his friends that he had money of his own. I think
that his meanness was due to naked fear; and it came as a
revelation when I left a message in Wheeler's restaurant at midday
to find him already seated at the bar tucking into oysters and the
house Chablis. My appearance there could hardly have been less
welcome, for he realised that the news of what I had seen would
reverberate through Soho, as it did, greeted with astonishment:
'Do you think he does that *every* morning?'

That was an unfortunate slip. More typical was the morning when he entered the French carrying a crumpled suit which Archer glared at edgily.

'What are you doing with that?'

Deakin rounded without a second's hesitation. 'What do you think I'm doing?' he demanded angrily. 'I'm pawning it. I have to pay my rent, don't I?'

'Dear me,' said Archer, 'I thought I paid that several days ago. Ah, well . . .' and produced two pound notes: 'You'd better have these.'

Deakin accepted them with an ill grace and allowed Archer to buy him a drink. A few minutes later when Archer had gone, Deakin told me to wait while he put his suit in the cleaners – 'as I was going to do all along!'

At such moments I should have felt sorry for Archer, except that he was not a man to feel pity for. He may have been a born victim but he was something of a grievance collector too. At this particular moment in the early fifties, he was at his most content, investing the last of his money in a splendid new bookshop to cater especially for Soho people at the Shaftesbury Avenue end of Greek Street. This was to be the biggest venture in his life, so he was living in the happiest of states – *anticipation*.

Phyllis

'Phyllis', also known as 'Rosie' because he wore a rose behind each ear, had been thrown out of the French earlier that day. He darted into the pubs of Soho in order to create a scene. Later, in a very rash moment I gave him half a crown, which meant that forever after if he saw me he made a dash towards me with a cry of joyful recognition: 'Mr Farson, Mr Farson, *dear*! Give me the price of a drink. Oh, well, give me the kiss of life.' He had a knack of appearing when I was trying to impress someone. His devastating screams and comments were broken off abruptly as he was thrown out, but at least the atmosphere had been enlivened.

Phyllis's real name was Timothy Cotter. Sometimes he'd appear horribly beaten up and people whispered that this had happened when he was arrested. This was not necessarily true, but his only 'fixed address' was Brixton Police Station and it was here that he died after one of his bouts of drunkenness. As he had no relatives and no friends, a pauper's funeral was imminent, but then a wonderful thing happened. The street traders of Berwick Street market took over the responsibility, decorating their stalls with flowers and photographs of Phyllis in order to raise the money to 'send him off' in style. 'The stalls were startling,' Deakin told me, 'like primitive Greek shrines.' Two hundred pounds were raised and Phyllis enjoyed a moment of posthumous approval as the *Daily Mirror* described him as 'an incredibly kind man and well-loved by everybody. His endless kindness, especially to children, made him a very popular figure.'

How death transforms! Phyllis ran errands for the traders and may have presented a different face to them, but he was a fearful nuisance too, barred from most of the pubs in Soho, and also rather frightening. I began to feel that behind the madness lay a devilish perception, that a sane man lurked inside the freak. On hangover mornings, I am ashamed to admit that I crossed the street to avoid him, warned by his shrill progress towards me. Yet he was so eccentric, with every shred of conventionality abandoned, that he was admirable too. No one wanted to know him when he made his screaming appearance in the doorway but they wanted to be in at the death. Two thousand people turned up for the funeral, lavishly organised by the traders as if he was the last Chicago gangster, and doffed their hats as the flower-laden coffin passed by *en route* to the cemetery. One news photo showed a tiresome adversary, who also wore flowers in his ears, saluting both the cortège and the camera. 'We won't see the like of him again,' the crowd said, uttering all the usual dishonest euphemisms when someone disconcerting dies.

2.00 p.m. On to Wheeler's

'I think this is going to be one of the good days,' said Deakin. 'Look who's just come in.' Opening his mouth in that grisly grimace which passed for a smile, Deakin nodded to a man on the far side of the bar who came over to join us.

'What are you having to drink?' he asked. He wore a well-cut grey suit and an open-necked shirt, with an effect that was simultaneously smart and casual. He was one of the few people I have met who had pronounced jowls; he walked over with the cautious tread of a first-class passenger venturing out on deck in a high sea. His voice was mocking and his laugh so infectious that I started laughing too when he announced, 'The most extraordinary thing has happened to me.'

'Well,' he continued, once the drinks were served. He tugged at the collar of his shirt as if he could hardly credit it himself, and enunciated his words carefully. 'I was in the Westminster Bank yesterday and a perfect stranger came up and asked me the way to Harrods. Well, really. . . !' He tugged at his collar again and shook with laughter at such absurdity. 'He could have thought of a better excuse than *that*. Well, as a matter of fact, he was rather good-looking, very sunburnt, rather fascist. He told me that he was a colonel in the army in South Africa, and then he asked me to lunch. He took me to the Ritz!'

This was greeted by a scream of laughter from Henrietta who had finished her lunch and joined us.

'Well, it really was too amazing. At the end of the meal he said he was going back to South Africa in the evening and would I like to come too. He said he'd pay all my expenses and do you know, I said "Yes". I thought I would like to go; after all, I've never been to the place. It might be quite interesting –who knows?' he shrugged. 'Well, there you are. But by the time the coffee arrived I thought better of it. After all, I knew nothing about him, so I said I'd changed my mind and was sorry but I couldn't go after all. I invented some excuse, I forget what it was.

'Well, he made the most fantastic scene! He threw his glass on the floor and shouted. He shouted the most filthy things at me. Of course the waiters behaved impeccably and picked up the plates again, but he went so far that I had to leave. Wasn't it an extraordinary thing to do?'

Having come to the end of the incident, he lost all interest: 'What's everyone having to drink?

Introductions are rare in Soho. Explanations in the American style – This is my husband Kellogg Q. Fairburn who works in real-estate and has given me three beautiful daughters – are even rarer, which is something to be thankful for; but even if Deakin had told me that Francis Bacon was a painter it would have meant little to me then. Though revered within a small circle he was scarcely recognised beyond it.

Francis Bacon turned to me with the attentiveness he reserved for strangers and asked – 'Shall we all go to Wheeler's for something to eat?'

This was the precedent for the next ten years when a chance meeting in the French led to a late lunch at Wheeler's, where we arrived at 2.30 p.m. just before the hot food finished. There were mornings when Deakin, Francis and myself laughed so spontaneously that people looked across enviously, as if they wished to touch us for luck. If I had paused in Soho before, I was stranded now.

I had discovered the key to Soho: that this is a place where friendships are forged for life because you share the same interests and are not hurled together as you might be in the army or a job. I was accepted because I was young and possessed a zest for living and that was enough. I also provided the perfect foil for Deakin's irreverence. Once someone accused him of corrupting me. 'Don't be ridiculous,' he snapped back. 'You cannot corrupt the incorruptible.' Paradoxically, I suspect that the incorruptible are the most vulnerable, but I was a willing victim. I had joined the Soho club.

Lunch at Wheeler's

Though few people called Archer or Deakin by their Christian names, Francis has always been Francis to everyone, including the waiters who welcomed us as we entered the ground floor of Wheeler's in Old Compton Street. There are some rooms, and they are sadly few, which are wholly sympathetic either by design or happy accident and this was one of them. The front door – part of the green façade with the heading 'Oysters/WHEELER'S & CO./ Merchants' – opened into the restaurant with a long counter along the left-hand side, where a waiter in a white apron opened oysters at lightning speed, with decorative plates, prints and a signed animation by Walt Disney on the wall behind. There was a small bar with plush seats at the back, which was also tremendously congenial. The atmosphere of the restaurant itself was highly professional but unpretentious with plain wooden tables without table cloths; place-mats, cutlery and napkins; a pile of brown bread and butter and bowls of radishes and spring onions. The kitchen staff were mainly Chinese, controlled by an elderly man called Mr Song who never smiled, in spite of his name, and delighted Lucian Freud as he passed through on his way to the street when he finished at 3.00 p.m., with a dour 'Musn't glumble' when Lucian asked him how he was.

Wheeler's had particular panache in the fifties. Over the years the staff shared our triumphs and disasters, observed our high spirits and furious arguments, and became our friends. In return, we provided a sort of cabaret. All of this was due to the owner, Bernard Walsh, who started in his father's fish business by selling oysters in Whitstable and founded Wheeler's in Soho in 1929 as a small retail oyster shop, renting the entire house for £400 a year. Seeing the success of his oysters in London's top restaurants, he bought a few tables and chairs and served them to customers of his own. By the fifties, the large menu had expanded to include thirty-two ways of serving sole and lobster but still no vegetables apart from salad and a few boiled potatoes. When I took my grandmother there, she found this hard to accept and was positively crestfallen to learn that there were no ice-creams or puddings. Instead, Wheeler's excelled in the ultimate simplicity of fresh English seafood – even if the hot food was prepared by Chinamen. In the post-war depression, when British food was at its dreariest, Wheeler's was luxury.

In spite of its expansion, Wheeler's remained a one-man effort, reflecting Walsh's Edwardian ebullience, with a touch of Dickensian gusto too. A former dancer in the male chorus, he was now a heavyweight, though still light on his feet. He had twinkling blue eyes and spoke with exuberance and a slight, endearing lisp. He was passionate about horse-racing, both as an owner and a gambler, and a bon viveur, relishing good drink as well as food. He started the Thursday Club for his friends on an upstairs floor, subsidising their gargantuan appetites and thirsts out of his own profits. When a favourite customer finally settled a long overdue bill, he was known to send round a bottle of champagne as a sort of 'thank you'. And when a group of American tourists once objected to our outrageous language, he bristled with loyalty: 'I'd much prefer it if *you* would leave,' he told them, 'so please do so now. These are my close friends.'

His reputation extended to digging 2,000 lugworms in a tide and opening 1,000 oysters at lunch.

Curiously, although Wheeler's was expensive, it never seemed to daunt us. This was largely because Francis preferred the role of host. He might not have had the cash to pay for fish and chips, but he signed for the oysters and the house Chablis, settling when he sold a picture. This was part of the pecking order in Soho where it did not seem shameful to borrow half a crown because it could be your chance to be generous tomorrow.

One day even Francis needed money urgently and asked me if I knew of someone who would buy a large canvas based on the Velasquez portrait of Pope Innocent X. I persuaded my college friend who had shared a flat in Beauchamp Place to buy it, almost wrecking his marriage in the process, for his wife grew to loathe the purple figure which screamed in silence at the top of the stairs in their mews cottage. When I handed over £150 in notes, I was surprised when Francis gave me back £15 as my 'dealer's commission', for this was unexpected and seemed a fortune then. The figure involved shows how cheaply Bacon's work could have been acquired at that time; today, that Pope would fetch several hundred thousand.

Part of the excitement in knowing Francis in the early fifties was the sense that he was poised on the threshold of something truly remarkable. The most single-minded man I have known, he was biding his time, totally consistent, totally alone, totally original.

Francis Bacon

Born in Dublin of English parents forty-two years earlier, he had spent a fleeting period at school at Cheltenham but he was hardly a conventional boy. His father put him in the care of an uncle who ran a racing stable in the hope that this 'would make a man of him'. Luckily for Francis, the sportive uncle took his nineteen-year-old nephew to Berlin, where the decadence in 1927 delighted them both. Francis returned there later but the next important influence on his life was when he saw an exhibition by Picasso in Paris, which encouraged him to become a painter. He taught himself and has never regretted the lack of a formal training in draughtsmanship: 'One sees the people who have been taught, who are painting nowadays. What are they doing? After all, they never make anything new, they just go back to a kind of academic drawing which would have been much better done by artists in the past.' When he stood in for John Minton for two or three months at the Royal College of Art, he realised that he could not teach anything: 'All I could do was go there, for two days a week, and if the students

wanted someone to talk to, I was there.' Even so, he was influenced
by the older Australian painter, Roy de Maistre, and was a regular
visitor at his studio off Ebury Street.

He spent a brief spell working in a wholesale shop for women's
clothes in Poland Street in Soho: 'I knew nothing about the
business; they more or less employed me just to answer the
telephone.' He disliked his employer so intensely that he spent
most of his working day composing letters of abuse and then
tearing them up, until the afternoon when he included one by
accident in the office post and was sacked on the spot.

After inserting an advertisement in *The Times*, giving himself an
excellent reference on the phone, he worked briefly as a 'gentleman's gentleman' until his gentleman saw him dining at the next
table in the Ritz on his evening off and also sacked him.

Francis has admitted to Miriam Gross that he was not at all
honest when young. 'I used to steal money from my father
whenever I could and I was always taking rooms in London and
then disappearing – not paying the rent, not being able to pay it.
What's called morality has grown on me with age. But in those
days I managed to get by on petty theft and on living off people.'

His lack of so-called morality was in the Bohemian tradition but
an exceptional discipline ran parallel, as he felt his way with his
painting and modernistic furniture, some of which was bought by
the Conservative politician, R. A. Butler. There were several
influential visitors to Roy de Maistre's Ebury studio: Patrick
White, Henry Moore, and Douglas Cooper, who commissioned
Francis to design an art deco rug and some tubular chairs which he
showed off to his friends in later years as objects of ridicule.
Graham Sutherland's influence was the greatest of all. Though
people tend to forget this, Francis held his first one-man show in
1934 at the Transition Gallery in the basement of Sunderland
House in Curzon Street, and his *Crucifixion*, painted the previous
year, was reproduced by Herbert Read in his book *Art Now* and
bought by Sir Michael Sadler. In 1937 Francis contributed three
paintings to the 'Young British Painters' Exhibition at Agnew's,

along with Graham Sutherland, Victor Passmore, John Piper and Roy de Maistre, after which he destroyed most of his work.

Graham and Kathy Sutherland became close friends of mine and told me of his historic win at Monte Carlo when he took them to the Hotel de Paris for one of the grandest dinners of their lives.

'You must go back to England,' they beseeched him, 'or give the money to someone to take it back for you. You've won enough never to worry again.'

The prospect appalled him: 'I don't want to be cushioned against the future,' he replied, and after paying a year's rent for a villa, with a massive deposit at his favourite delicatessen, he returned to the Casino to lose the rest.

Bacon's war service could not be described as distinguished. Legend has it that when he received his call-up papers he hired an Alsatian dog from Harrods and slept beside it overnight. As he suffers from asthma, and happens to be allergic to dogs, he was gasping for breath by the time he reported for his medical the next morning and was rejected as unfit.

Instead, Francis joined the ARP (Air Raid Precaution) and indulged his obsession for gambling by fronting an illegal gaming club in his spacious South Kensington studio where his old nanny lent a touch of respectability by looking after the coats and hats.

When we met in 1951 he was still living in South Kensington. Outside a narrow section of the art world, he was virtually unknown, though recognised by his fellow-artists in Soho, including John Minton, Rodrigo Moynihan and Lucian Freud, as a shattering new talent. The turning point had occurred at the Lefevre Gallery six years earlier when *Three Studies for the Base of a Crucifixion* were added without warning to an exhibition which included work by Henry Moore, Matthew Smith and Graham Sutherland. John Russell has described the impact: 'Visitors tempted to that gallery by the already familiar name of Graham Sutherland were brought up short by images so unrelievedly awful that the mind shut with a snap at the sight of them . . . these figures had an anatomy half-human, half-animal . . . they were equipped to probe, bite and suck . . . two at least of them were sightless. One was unpleasantly bandaged. They caused a total consternation.' Francis himself insists that nothing in his work mattered before the *Three Studies*, which were bought by the Tate in 1953 and can be seen there today.

In spite of their impact, Francis Bacon's reputation was still confined to a small circle of friends. He continued to exhibit at minor galleries like the Hanover, where a private view was a mixture of reverence and revelry with plenty of wine, plenty of friends and John Deakin telling everyone that *he* thought the paintings were simply marvellous, with the implication that he alone could understand them. Always the perfect host, Francis smiled eagerly throughout, welcoming friends and strangers alike. The presentation might have been modest, with a six-page catalogue in black and white, but on 20 March 1957 the exhibition included the four studies of Van Gogh with their brilliant outbursts of colour and the *Study for Figure V*. The latter had been bought the year before by Robert and Lisa Sainsbury, who were probably his leading patrons; they also bought the first study of Van Gogh.

One evening Francis took me to the Sainsburys' home for a drink. I was slightly overwhelmed by the hushed opulence and such treasures as the Degas sculpture of a little ballet girl wearing a real net tutu: *Petite Danseuse de Quatorze Ans*. Their son was kind enough to show me the rest of their remarkable collection and as we came downstairs I noticed a Bacon portrait and searched for the right thing to say, failing absymally as most people do on such occasions. 'That really is magnificent,' I floundered. 'What an amazing likeness of your father.'

'Yes,' replied their son coldly, 'except that it happens to be my mother.'

Most of the Sainsburys' collection can be seen at their Centre for Visual Arts at the University of East Anglia today, including the Degas sculpture and the Bacon *Study for Portrait of Van Gogh*. Also, his *Three Studies for Portrait of Isobel Rawsthorne* (1965). By a happy coincidence, or the shrewdness of the Sainsburys, the Centre also contains the bronze head – *Tête d'Isabelle* – sculpted by Giacometti.

Francis talked in Mayfair cockney, an exaggerated whine with a note of self-mockery – 'I'm not the fool I seem' – sometimes lapsing into schoolboy French – '*Pas de tout, chérie*'. The difficulty with describing Francis lies in capturing his enunciation, which could make a nondescript remark hilarious. 'I'm just a simple idiot' looks crass in cold print yet it seemed devastatingly funny when he pronounced it 'iddy-ott'. When we celebrated his birthday at L'Escargot, he eyed the succulent slices of lamb served in a rich sauce and exclaimed, 'I do hope they don't give me *gravy* on mine,' investing that word with all the dolefulness of the Victorian workhouse. Throwing a pocket mirror on the floor of the Colony with disdain, he echoed Talullah Bankhead's sister – 'They certainly don't make mirrors like they used to' – and poured his bottle of champagne into the glasses of his friends with the Edwardian toast: 'Champagne to your real friends, real pain for your sham friends', followed by the beaming addition of 'Cheery-ho!'

His idiosyncratic manner made him enchanting company but anyone attempting to write about Francis Bacon will confirm the hazards involved. The late Frank Norman tried to, but abandoned the contest after trailing Francis for several days around the bars and restaurants of Soho. He wrote to me later:

I felt like a spy. He spoke marvellously about Berlin in the 1920s but things deteriorated and I was reduced to keeping my ears open, nipping into the lavatory to scribble notes on bits of toilet paper! In the morning I'd find all these screwed-up pieces in my pocket scrawled in a barely legible hand with such choice remarks as: 'I have never had any love in the whole of my life – and what's more I don't want any. All I do is cast my rod into the sewers of despair and see what I come up with this time.' I was greatly relieved when the whole thing petered out.

I can hear Bacon's voice ringing with ridicule: 'Despair? I have grown accustomed to its face, oysters and despair – the diet of my life,' then a burst of laughter followed by the declaration 'I don't believe in tragedy.' Conversely, he could become serious in an instant: 'I want, very, very much to do the thing that Valéry said – to give the sensation without the boredom of its conveyance,' or 'If you can say it, don't paint it.'

One afternoon, talking generally about the passivity of people though not in a sexual context, Francis remarked: 'Don't you realise, 95 per cent of people are passive, waiting to be entertained.'

This was a new idea to me, unaware that my new drinking companions were the exceptions, the puppet-masters who jerked the strings which brought the marionettes to life. Many years later I reminded Francis of this remark and he swung round apparently displeased: 'Did I really say that? How stupid of me.' There was the briefest pause before he added: 'I should have said 99½ per cent.'

Three years before I met Francis Bacon, Brian Howard had taken him to the Colony Room at 41 Dean Street on the day before it opened, and introduced him to the owner, Muriel Belcher. They liked each other instantly and she offered him £10 and free drinks if he brought big-spending cutsomers to her club. So Bacon had risen from self-confessed petty thief to tout for Miss Belcher. It was a considerable step forward.

'Muriel's' was our next destination, after Francis signed the bill at Wheeler's.

3.00 p.m. The Day Goes On at The Colony

'Members only!'

Muriel Belcher perched on her corner stool next to the door, beady-eyed and imperial. The name of the Colony Room had suggested something grand but this was belied by the dustbins below and the filthy, ill-lit stairs. The club proved to be little more than a small and shabby room with a telephone and a lavatory at the back, and a battered upright piano, but Miss Belcher was grandeur personified. Chin tilted upwards, cigarette in raised hand, she gave an impression of haughtiness, an eagle surveying the carrion of her membership. Her black hair was combed back severely and her strong Jewish features tempted several artists to paint her, including Francis Bacon who told me, 'She's a very beautiful woman. It's as simple as that.'

Why did Francis go there so often? 'Because it's different from anywhere else. She has a tremendous ability to create an atmosphere of ease. After all, that's what we all want, isn't it? A place to go to where one feels free and easy.'

Her warning shriek of 'Members only!' was not an idle one; even football supporters, wandering in by mistake, did not argue with her. She was strict on this and rightly so, for she maintained the balance of the club with the skill of a great hostess, encouraging a marvellous mix of people, ranging from titled folk to impoverished artists. She knew nothing about painting but she liked painters because they created fun and if they were unable to pay for their drinks they charmed others into doing so. In the early fifties the club was used regularly by John Minton, Lucian Freud, Frank Auerbach, Michael Andrews and Francis Bacon to whom it was home. By instinct, rather than calculation, Muriel attracted the liveliest artistic talent in England in the fifties.

It did not matter to her if you were penniless, but she was ruthless with those who were reasonably rich yet mean. 'Open your bead-bag, Lottie,' she'd cry, 'and we'll all have a drink with this vision of loveliness,' and the reluctant man was forced to buy a round before he left the club, never to been seen again. Conversely, her smile was almost a curtsey when confronted by wealth. On a subsequent visit I was surprised to see her take no interest in a woman who was deep in conversation in the corner. I had recognised her at once. After she had gone, I asked Muriel if she had known who she was.

'That drab little number in the raincoat with the sallow skin?'

'That was Olga Deterding, probably the richest woman in the world.'

'Really!' gasped Muriel with new admiration. 'It's funny, but now you say that her complexion seems more radiant and her hair has gained a new lustre. Yes, a very attractive number, that little Miss Deterding.'

The Colony Room was everything I hoped for. To start with I was shocked by Muriel's language, which caused her to be barred from a Chinese restaurant in Limehouse, and I was astounded when she greeted Deakin, 'And how are you, girl?' But I grew to relish her habit of greeting middle-aged men as 'Miss' and noticed that they seemed to welcome such attention. The most inappropriate men were referred to as if they were women: Hitler was dismissed as 'Miss Hitler', and she described Shaw, on his death, as 'a clever little woman'. A charming elderly man called Leonard Blackett came to the Colony every evening after his day's work in the City and I assume that he received free drinks though most of his richer contemporaries had died. He lent a touch of apparent respectability, and was referred to with admiration as 'a gallant little woman in the Somme'. Francis was known as 'daughter'.

Once I asked who her favourite customers were; though I should have known the answer. 'Those that spend the most, *deah*!' But if you were entertaining that did not matter for the drinks would flow around you. Next to those who were mean, she disliked the bores, scenting them out immediately.

One afternoon when the club was comparatively quiet, the door opened and an inoffensive, though mousey, man peered round to ask if his friends had arrived.

With the sudden venom of a child who scents a weaker prey, she gave a snort of disapproval: 'I don't think you're likely to find any of your friends in *my* club.'

'But we arranged to meet,' the man stammered. I recognised him now as the distinguished, if earnest, editor of a literary magazine, but even if Muriel had known this she would not have been impressed.

Turning to the rest of us with a disdainful toss of her head, she declared, 'She's not a pretty little lady is she?'

The editor quivered with impotent rage. 'I've never been so insulted in my life.'

'On your way, Lottie,' she replied, taking hold of the door, 'or I'll give you a fourpenny one.'

She was so rude to John Braine, crying out 'There's plenty of room at her top!', that he started legal action against her until his solicitor urged him not to be so silly; and she was so insulting to Barry Humphries before he became Dame Edna or Sir Les that he never set foot in her club again, and he speaks of it bitterly today as one of the nastiest places he has known. All of this makes her sound like a monster, but she could be immensely kind and perceptive, qualities recognised by Paul Potts, a formidable Soho personality himself with the oval head of a Pope and the wicked smile of an unfrocked priest. Disgracefully underrated, his books, *Dante Called You Beatrice*, *To Keep a Promise*, and *Invitation to a Sacrament*, contain some of the most astute statements of our time; but Paul's abrasiveness is not moulded to fashion and he has suffered accordingly, though praised by George Orwell, T. S. Eliot and Sean O'Casey. He wrote me a beautiful letter in which he tried to sum up Muriel's qualities:

> I suppose what makes her so difficult to describe is her originality, a kind of non-ecclesiastical cardinal or perhaps a delinquent saint. She is a natural procurer whether it be the Bacon for the eggs or a date for a girl friend. The relatively small room which is her domain and where she is an absolute sovereign must be one of the most unique rooms anywhere. It is not like other clubs at all, more like a continuous cocktail party. It is the sort of place where you can't get much for ten bob but you can get an awful lot for nothing. Once you're in you're in; the poor and the private get treated just as well as the rich and famous. But if she does not like you – you've had it. She is autocratic as the Dalai Lama and as kind as Sophie Tucker.

Paul concluded witch a series of bull's-eyes: 'She could have run a great hospital if she had wanted to. She certainly could have been a successful impresario. But drink and conversation are her materials and she brought them together and has caused a huge amount of happiness to come people's way.'

When I crept round that door in my early twenties, I thought that Muriel and her members were the most fascinating people I had ever met. I still do.

Why did I and so many others make this place our second home? The answer is simple: we could be ourselves, and that is one of the hardest things to achieve in life.

If Muriel had a genius as a club-owner, as I believe she did, it was her ability to mix all sorts of people, so that the Colony was never typed or predictable. Paul regarded her as Soho royalty and claimed that 'an eighteenth-century duchess would recognise in her a sister'. Outside the club she looked like a night-animal caught in the glare of daylight as it scurried over the asphalt, yet I could picture her at home in Chatsworth. She held court at the Colony with her own aristocracy: Lord May; the Lady Rose MacLaren, one of the famous Paget sisters whose father was the Marquis of Anglesey and whose aunt was Lady Diana Cooper; Tim Willoughby and his sister Jane; the Hon. Garech Browne.

The Colony even featured in a *Millionaire's Diary* alongside six other clubs including Boodle's and White's, though the mention was retracted.

In those early days there was a Cypriot club upstairs which attracted a colourful mix of beatniks, layabouts, and minor villains. Unsuspecting guests on their first visit to the Colony were startled to step across unconscious bodies and past policewomen interviewing grey-faced teenage girls, and to have to press themselves against the wall as one man pursued another into the street brandishing a knife.

I was told that a previous restaurant downstairs, under different management, became besieged by rats. As she counted the takings one evening at closing time, Muriel noticed four red eyes glaring at her from a corner of the room.

'You two can fuck off,' she told them. But as Muriel was a kind woman she explained: 'You see, I've called last orders. Anyhow you're not members.' She opened the door and the rats left without argument.

Muriel Belcher

Like most people in Soho, Muriel rarely referred to her background, which was highly respectable. She was born in Birmingham, which explains her dislike of provincials: 'They're all such fucking bores. Oh, except that nice cousin of mine that lives in Cheshire. Can't think what his name is.' Her parents were rich Portuguese Jews who owned the Alexandra Theatre and she had 'one nice brother who died'. 'My nanny was a real bastard and the governess would have had more hair on her chin than Che Guevara except that she shaved every day. I loathed my fucking old father but loved my mother dearly. My brother, mother and I came to live in London in 1937 after my father died and that was freedom for us all.' A year later she started a club called the Music Box in Leicester Place in partnership with Dolly Myers. This catered for the last gasp of the Bright Young Things, such as Elvira Barney: 'I found her enchanting. She fell in love with a pouf called Spider and later killed him. But she had what I'd call friends in high places, and wasn't convicted. She'd burst into the club and make a scene: "I've shot one bugger and got away with it, so don't think I'd hesitate to shoot another." '

In the war the Music Box became a famous theatrical rendezvous, but Dolly married a man called Alf and one of them allegedly pushed the other down the stairs to his or her death, I forget which, and its days as a rendezvous were over. By this time Muriel had moved on, opening the Colony on 15 December 1948. Her mother had died earlier that year which might have given her the means to do so. Christopher Kininmouth said that it was so empty that first afternoon that they played dice along the counter. The stools were covered in leopard-skin and the bar adorned with bamboo. The bamboo was there when I arrived, but the carpet was threadbare and the leopard-skins had gone.

I have known numerous parodies of Muriel Belcher: equally formidable ladies – sometimes wearing large hats – who managed similar clubs with the authority of Madams, but they never approached her style. They might have shared her shrewdness, but not her dignity. They tried to be 'characters' and many of their members were fooled, but they were of a lesser calibre. Muriel was an original.

She was also a beauty. There is a photograph of her taken by Angus MacBean in the forties in which she resembled Hedy Lamarr. When I knew her better, I asked about the rumour that a South American diplomat had fallen in love with her. 'Perfectly true, deah. I did have a Colombian gentleman who was in love with me. I don't know how it started – or ended.' Asked about the other loves of her life, men or women, she replied tersely – 'I'm glad to say plenty of both' – but would not say more. When I knew her, her single love was her West Indian friend Carmel who provided the friction with her obsessive gambling at which she seemed singularly unlucky. At one point they broke up and Carmel returned to Jamaica, only to regret it bitterly, phoning Muriel one night with the wistful wail: 'I wanna come home.'

'You *are* home, cunty,' said Muriel, putting the phone down, but it was not long before Carmel was back.

Muriel's humour, and that of many of the older members of the Colony, like Avril Gay, was a form of high camp left over from the thirties. Words ended in '-kins', as in 'blissikins', or in '-ette' as in 'Would you like a drinkette?'

However turbulent or crowded the Colony became, Muriel absorbed the scene, apparently with eyes at the back of her head. When Deakin bent down to stroke a charming white husky dog which someone had brought to the club, she cried out a warning, even though she was deep in conversation at the bar:

'Hold on to your sled, gal, or that one will bum a free ride to Alaska.'

The dog happened to look up with a bemused expression at that precise moment and Muriel turned to us triumphantly: 'Glad to see she's got the message!'

Muriel's feelings towards John Deakin were ambivalent. Matters came to a head after she took over the charity I had started for children suffering from muscular dystrophy and other handicaps, at Elmfield School. My clumsy efforts were replaced by a full-scale production as members were enlisted to contribute money. Private 'balls' were held late at night to raise funds. Eventually, coachloads were to descend on the startled school, shattering the peace and quiet, with George Melly and Annie Ross conscripted to provide a cabaret. But the first of the parties for the children was held in the basement of the Italian trattoria below the Colony, where Muriel invited the members who had volunteered to have lunch beforehand. As a wise precaution, no spirits were allowed though vast quantities of red wine were knocked back at alarming speed in order to break the tension as we waited for the children to arrive. When they did so, there were no embarrassed pauses and they were plainly puzzled or entranced by the hubbub which greeted them. I still remember one moment from that frenetic afternoon:

'Decks of cards, I need decks of cards,' cried the conjuror.

'Speak for yourself, Kate,' came Muriel Belcher's voice, 'I need Dexedrine.'

When the party came to an end the children were carried outside, clutching their expensive presents, though some insisted on taking the painful steps themselves. As their coach turned the corner with the children waving back to the Colony members standing shaken in the deserted Sunday Soho street, it was hard to say who had gained the most.

Deakin was conspicuous in his absence. Either he had been considered unsuitable, or he had kept away of his own accord, which seemed more likely. Unfortunately, his comments were expressed too loudly and winged their way swiftly back to the club. 'Don't kid me,' he was heard to say, 'where do you think the money went to which was raised from those so-called balls? Straight into Miss Mu's pocket.' Muriel would tolerate a great deal – even the charge of embezzlement could be laughed away – but the subject of the children was sacred and he was not forgiven.

Colin MacInnes

Colin MacInnes usually made a late appearance in the Colony, pushing the door open abruptly as if it had done him some injustice. He entered the room with the arrogance of a ringmaster, trailing the inevitable coloured man behind him.

'Take your hat off,' Colin ordered him, 'and say good afternoon to Miss Belcher. Go and sit in the corner over there –and *don't* smoke.'

Ian Board worked behind the bar and remembers Colin's astonishing rudeness to his black friends – 'And the extraordinary thing was that they obeyed him! He wouldn't have got away with it today.'

Surprisingly, Colin's perceptiveness as a writer failed him when he described Muriel, disguised as Mabel, in his essay for *Encounter* (March 1957), 'See You at Mabel's.' This essay reflected his personal preference for the afternoon club rather than the pub: 'A lot of drinkers dislike public houses very much.' The club offered greater privacy and even stimulated Colin's requisite of danger because clubs were barely tolerated within the letter of the law and liable to be raided at any moment in case they infringed it. In his *Encounter* article, Colin wrote:

These clubs conform more or less . . . yet it is clear that Mabel's was not the kind of club imagined by the legislator, and that she and her resourceful colleagues conduct their clubs in ways quite different from those that were intended. In a nutshell, the paradox is this: though hundreds of these places are technically 'members' clubs, they belong in fact more absolutely to individual owners than any public house does to its licensee.

As everyone knew, the afternoon clubs were a means of breaking our insane licensing laws by providing places where people could drink as much as they wanted and pay the owners handsomely for doing so.

This was why the personality of the club-owner was all important.

And what of Mabel's place? [as Colin referred to Muriel's] Mabel's a character often met with in films and fiction, but oh! so rarely in reality: the platinum-tough girl with a heart of gold. Sharp, hard, ruthless and aggressive, she's generous, forgiving, considerate and rather shy. Quite ignorant of the inner operations of the professional worlds of all her members, she can nevertheless assess, with uncanny accuracy, their intrinsic talents and current reputations. In appearance she's a *belle laide*, bulky and perpetually radiant. Her conversation's witty and salacious, her capacity for absorbing spirits without ill effect apparently limitless. She's always glad to see you ('Sweetie! Come and kiss mother! You're a cup of tea!'), and just as glad, when time comes to tot the takings, to see you go.

Yet, in writing about her as a composite character, Colin missed Muriel's outstanding quality – her originality. But he did catch that uneasy sense of guilt as we drank away the afternoon, especially if the sun was shining outside.

Of course the spell of the drinking club is partly morbid. To sit in Mabel's place, with the curtains drawn at 4 p.m. on a sunny afternoon, sipping expensive poison and gossiping one's life away, has the futile fascination of forbidden fruit: the heady intoxication of a bogus Baudelairian romantic evil. As the gins slip down your throat, and the dim electrics shine on the potted plants and on Mabel's lurid colour scheme of emerald green and gold, you feel like the fish in the tank above the cash-register – swimming aimlessly among artificial water-weeds, mindless in warm water.

Colin appealed to Muriel's sense of humour. She enjoyed friction and Colin delighted in his rudeness.

We were introduced in the Colony, and spoke briefly, so a few days later I was pleased to see him sitting by himself in the empty restaurant car of a train and went up to him eagerly, delighted to have someone to talk to.

'Look, Mister,' he snarled, with a dangerous glint in his half-closed eyes, 'because we've met that doesn't mean you're allowed to talk to me.' The words came like a slap in the face and I must have looked so hurt as I withdrew that even Colin was regretful and tried to make amends afterwards, though neither of us referred to the incident. The 'amends' came in the form of helpful, sometimes anonymous write-ups which I had the sense to acknowledge with barely a hint of recognition as I nodded to him across the Colony Room. Colin recoiled from thanks.

I remained wary, for I suspected that he took a surly pleasure in his rudeness as a form of self-laceration. One afternoon I was in the Colony drinking with one of the nicest people I have known: his face was that of a born comic with boot-brush hair and tombstone teeth, and his good nature should have been obvious to anyone. Hearing our laughter Colin lurched over with his usual snarl and I introduced them reluctantly.

'My God!' Colin exclaimed, 'you must be the ugliest man I've ever seen.'

I guffawed with the pretence that this was a form of endearment and tried to repair the damage as Colin moved on to upset someone else, but I was not sucessful.

Why did Colin behave like this? Curiously, I think he enjoyed the bad behaviour which finally had him recalled from a British Council tour of Africa. Henrietta Law described him: 'awkward, not vicious, he was playful so long as you kicked him back on course.' Even so, he left a lot of troubled water in his wake.

Frank Norman

Frank Norman was another writer who frequented the Colony, though he wrote to me years later: 'I don't have to tell you about Muriel's swift harsh judgements of people. Goodness, how friendly she was towards me in the early sixties when *Fings* was going great guns at the Garrick. And then how hostile after *Kayf Up West* flopped and I grew up! She even refused to appear with that tubby cockney director whose name escapes me.' (He was the late Charlie Squires.) This is surprising for it seemed to me that Muriel was loyal throughout the worst of times as well as the best, and this was one of her qualities. Of course she *preferred* you to be successful, and there had been a time when Frank cavorted through Soho with Brendan Behan scattering fivers in the air. When times grew leaner, Frank could become more ponderous as a form of self-justification, and I suspect it was this that she resented.

Usually Frank was fun, with none of the dreary introspection of those who have brushed with the law and suffer from a sense of injustice. He knew the value of time, having served it, and it ran out far too soon. He was the classic example of a young man who achieves a great success too early. His later plays flopped, he quarrelled with Joan Littlewood over the production of *Costa Packet*, and was unable to place a comedy he had written called *Rough Trade*, 'really more about the decline and imminent fall of Soho than it is about club life,' he wrote to me in 1974, though 'a certain drinking club, not 100 yards from Oxford Circus, could in some respects be recognisable.'

When he wrote about his 'manor' and Soho in particular, he made the words dance. With his knowledge of and affection for petty villains, he could have been the Damon Runyon of Soho but he turned to writing rather turgid detective stories instead in the struggle to earn money. Luckily, he enjoyed one last glorious stroke of luck, in meeting Geraldine who became his wife; theirs was a lovely fusion of opposites, for she was well-educated and slightly grand, the sales correspondent for *The Times*, and he was the razor-scarred orphan from Dr Barnado's and Wandsworth

gaol. She saw him sitting next to the large stork ashtray in Muriel's
and told me that she met him later when she was dining at the
Trattoria Terrazza (in some versions she changed it to the
Dumpling Inn) and he lurched over, demanding a light for his
'ciggy', and collapsed over the table. 'It was love at first sight!' she
remembers. 'We laughed a lot that night and we carried on
laughing most of the time for eleven years and nine months, which
is a very good run but painfully short for a happy marriage.' Frank
was fifty when he died of Hodgkin's disease two days before
Christmas in 1980.

4.30 p.m. Next Stop

The Caves de France

Next door to the Colony was the Caves de France. The Colony
considered itself superior and Muriel looked askance when her
members deserted to the Caves, regarding this as a form of
betrayal. Francis, always a creature of habit, seldom crossed the
boundary; but following his falling-out with Muriel, John Deakin
made it his afternoon stop and it was my next destination that day.

The Caves de France was a long, low room on ground level. It
was so dark when I walked in from Dean Street that it took several
seconds for my eyes to adjust and penetrate the clouds of cigarette
smoke. In many ways this was the most astonishing place in Soho
and the closest to Bohemia.

Membership was perfunctory. There was a time when a young
wrestler with the head of a Greek god stopped strangers and asked
them, 'Can I help you? This is a member's club, you know?' but I
never saw a membership card and anyone with style could have
talked themselves in if they had dared to infiltrate such a close-knit
group of people who were fiercely self-contained.

Yet the membership was totally mixed and classless, and
changed according to the time of day. Though cigarette ends

patterned the floor, and wine had stained the furniture, the room was sympathetic, with a long bar on the left-hand side (which has given me a taste for high stools ever since) and tables and chairs along the other side. This wall was hung with staggeringly bad paintings of various views with a sign informing the viewer that these were the work of the Baron von Schine and were very definitely for sale. Underneath was a dubious list of the international galleries where the Baron had exhibited; and slumped even lower was the Baron himself, usually fast asleep with his mouth wide open. The Baron was an upright old gentleman with a purple face who wore a monocle, though seldom a collar or tie, and occasionally barked out military commands at no one in particular. He never sold a painting, he had never been to Eton as he claimed, and he infuriated the barmen by changing his pictures around continuously with sighs of admiration.

The bar staff consisted of the owner, Philippe; a genteel French-woman who looked thoroughly bemused by the behaviour of her clientele, as well she might; a stocky, youngish ex-petty officer called Frank who looked after the members with exemplary patience as if he were the warden of a remand home for delinquent adults; and Secundo Primera, the brother of Primo, whose mother apparently had difficulty in thinking up first names for her sons, who worked behind the bar with a huge, soft smile.

Although Muriel disapproved of Colony members frequenting the Caves, it nevertheless served a purpose by accepting her rejects. My father, Negley Farson, wrote that he had a preference for 'hurt people' and he would have found them in abundance at the Caves. Here were rejects of every kind: the drifters, the shabby genteel, those who had known better times. There were eyes guilty at knowing defeat, ravaged faces barely crowned with thinning hair, and musty clothes which needed changing, judging by their smell. Elaine Dundy, who was Ken Tynan's first wife, described it in her novel *The Old Man and Me* as 'a sort of coal-hole in the heart of Soho that is open every afternoon, a dead-ended subterranean tunnel . . . an atmosphere almost solid with failure.'

She failed to see the joy.

She failed to appreciate the good humour which overcame the failure. Every town should have a Caves de France, for such a meeting-place where people can unite and forget their vulnerabilities in the solace of drink and companionship is as necessary to a community as a church. Just as the early music hall enlivened people's evenings, so the Caves was the antidote to the loneliness of long afternoons. If there was an air of desperation, it was the desperation of defiance.

Of course there were solitaries, too – an old French lady who kept a silent vigil beside a glass of lager, with all the dejection of Degas's couple in *L'Absinthe*, and the girl I had seen in the French with the white face and the orange hair – but they were the ghosts at a timeless party. Again, because the 'membership' was so mixed there was an undercurrent of keen excitement. By today's standards, the level of wit and conversation in the Caves would rank with that of the Café Royal or the Algonquin in their heyday. But the Caves de France has gone and today's alternative is the television set, hour after hour after hour.

Nina Hamnett

Nina went to the Caves. Though she had been and still was a friend of Muriel, she was no longer tolerated in the Colony where the sniffier members might have objected to her language, apart from the slight, lingering smell after she wet herself. Nina Hamnett had known everyone once, as she related in her autobiography *Naked Torso* (named after the sculpture of herself by Gaudier-Brzeska – 'I'm in the V & A with my left tit knocked off'). In it she recalled her carefree life in Paris before the war when she was a famous model – 'Modigliani said I had the best tits in Europe' – and seemed to be everybody's friend – including Aleister Crowley's until he sued her in 1934 when she accused him in her book of practising black magic in Sicily and of being connected with the disappearance of a baby. Though worse accusations had been made against him before, Crowley expected handsome damages but the judge summed up against him – 'I have never heard such dreadful, horrible, blasphemous abominable stuff.'

Naked Torso is often an infuriating book, with its passing glimpses of the famous – 'Picasso stopped at our table to say how nice I was looking' (or flattering words to that effect). Remembering her gallant though anxious appearance at the Caves, a beret cocked on the side of her head, and a chuckle as she hoisted herself on the bar stool, when I met her I had expected someone more abrasive.

'You couldn't buy me a drink could you, love?' she'd gasp, which I did gladly, with the last remnants of the English public schoolboy I had been. Nina had echoes of upper-class respectability herself: her grandfather belonged to the Indian Civil service, as did mine, and though she was a derelict she retained a certain grandeur. Also, like many who are short of money, she was generous. When Bruce Bernard left home at the age of sixteen after a row with his mother, Nina put him up and made him fried-egg sandwiches: 'She was very kind but I got bed-bugs, and left.'

Nina boasted that she was 'the last of the Bohemians'; and she had more claim to the title than most. When she lived at L'Etoile in one of the few bedrooms above the restaurant in Charlotte Street, she was a leading figure in Fitzrovia and a drinking chum of Augustus John.

In the early fifties, Nina was still game but I could sense that her tide was ebbing. In earlier years, she had filled the hours until they overflowed and now she was having to settle the debt. She hawked around a portfolio of drawings and rattled her tin tobacco box where she kept her money if she wanted to alert people in the pub that she needed a drink. She began to make scenes and shout obscenities and became rather well known to the police. Yet I remember her surrounded by friends.

In my preoccupation then with the present, I regret that I took so little interest in her past, though we had the bond that she had known and liked my father in the thirties, even hinting at a brief 'affair'. Otherwise, God forgive me, she was just an elderly drunk.

In 1947 she had been brought to court by her landlady who had tried to evict her, using in evidence the way that Nina misused the sink. 'A woman urinating in the sink? It is not possible!' exclaimed the magistrate, much to the amusement of Soho, but though the landlady lost the case, Nina had to move after a fire, and found two rooms in Westbourne Terrace near the Regent's Canal.

Though her paintings provide a valuable footnote to the period, hers was a minor talent compared to that of Edward Burra, her contemporary, and it is fair to say that Nina was more interesting than her pictures. Once I went round an exhibition upstairs in the Café Royal with Francis Bacon and Lucian Freud, who stopped at a painting which had caught their attention. Lucian looked at the label on the back and reported 'Sickert'. This set me wondering as we continued our circuit, and as we passed it again I rashly broke my silence, for I had not dared to venture an opinion before.

'If that's by Sickert,' I declared, 'he could never have painted a great picture.'

The two of them looked at me with irritation, so with the hope of proving my point I bent down and looked at the back for myself, emerging triumphantly with the tactless cry – 'It's not *by* Sickert, it's *of* Sickert, by Nina Hamnett!' They were not amused.

Nina did not scrounge for drinks; instead she asked for them outright. Gaston Berlemont (of the French) remembers that her constant demands for money enraged David Archer to such an extent that he lost his temper and refused to lend her the pittance she was seeking. Then, with characteristic remorse, he returned a few minutes later with a ten-shilling note plus the consolation of a bunch of flowers which he presented with an awkward flourish.

Once, trying to improve her appearance, she took her best grey dress to the cleaners – 'My dear, it just shrivelled up because of the gin soaked into it over the years. All they gave me back was a spoonful of dust.'

In 1953, after a drinking session at the Fitzroy, she fell and fractured a thigh bone which was troublesome enough, but when she returned to the hospital in 1954 to have the pin removed they bungled it, leaving one leg four inches shorter than the other, which explains why she was supported by a stick when I met her. The stick became her scaffolding, though she felt insulted when Augustus John recommended her to a home for aged artists. After a radio play about her life in Charlotte Street, which she considered a betrayal, she fell forty feet from her bedroom window, impaling herself on the railings below. She was taken to Paddington General Hospital, where Lucian Freud looked down with dismay at the emaciated figure barely sustained by tubes and traction, little more than 'a spoonful of dust' herself. He was joined by one of Nina's respectable relatives who had been summoned to her bedside and though she strongly disapproved of Nina's Bohemian lifestyle she did her best to be agreeable.

'Well,' she remarked brightly, staring at the ruins, 'still the same old Nina!' Nina's last words – and she was neither the first nor the last to use them – were, 'Why can't they let me die?'

She did so, on 16 December 1956, aged sixty-six, but I was so young that I thought of her as older than that.

The Two Roberts

'Get me a whisky will yer?' the man demanded in a thick Scottish accent. He looked wild and windswept with a white fall of cigarette ash on his coat, and banged the counter so fiercely that Secundo, so massive yet so gentle, winced with pain.

Another Scot on the stool beyond glared at me sourly: 'Why don't you fuck off?'

Like fallen rocks obstructing a cliff-path, the two Roberts sat at the bar blocking the way if you happened to pass. At first I was intimidated by their aggression; later I understood it; finally I admired it. Robert Colquhoun in particular had been a hope of British painting; by the fifties he had become the despair of numerous pubs and clubs, including Muriel's, where his brooding presence was unwelcome.

They were spending the last of their talent, yet like most reprobates they were puritanical at heart.

The dubious cliché that they were 'meant for each other' could be true. MacBryde was born in 1913 at Maybole in Ayrshire; Colquhoun a year later at Kilmarnock, twenty miles away. They met at the Glasgow School of Art in 1932: 'It was the usual course,' Colquhoun told me, 'but in those days it seemed pretty good. When we arrived they told us, "We can't make you artists; either you are or you're not, but we can teach you *how!*" '

After this they stayed together for most of their lives. Prizes and scholarships took them to Italy and France, and they lived in Paris when war was declared. Colquhoun enlisted in the Royal Medical Corps but MacBryde was rejected as medically unfit. He wrote to the army asking for his friend's release which came when Colquhoun collapsed from a convenient heart attack. The inseparable couple were reunited in London in 1941.

Colquhoun became famous after he was noticed by Duncan Macdonald of the Lefevre gallery who bullied, wheedled and fought for his first exhibition. His becoming fashionable coincided with the wartime recognition of other young painters: MacBryde, John Minton, Keith Vaughan, Michael Ayrton and John Craxton, all of whom prospered. Colquhoun explained his success with his usual sardonic humour: 'I s'pose people couldn't buy anything else.'

At his shows in 1946 and 1947 he sold more than half the pictures at prices ranging from £50 to £250. Then his luck ran out: the war ended, Macdonald died, and the policy of the Lefevre changed. Colquhoun's caustic personality did not please the prim gallery managers who took over and from then on the two Roberts had to waste valuable time trying to raise money in order to work.

Of the two, MacBryde was known to be the less cantankerous, while Colquhoun was the more satanic. I suspected that it was the other way round, especially when I caught Colquhoun off guard as he sat on the steps of the Golden Lion in Dean Street one morning waiting for the pub to open, as subdued as a shadow, and poignantly anxious to please. MacBryde kept home, wherever that happened to be, and did the ironing, accepting the lesser role of 'the servant to the great master' with pleasure, always promoting his friend's work to the detriment of his own. When I met them, their drinking had gained control over them and though Elizabeth Smart did her utmost to look after them at her home in Suffolk they made life so impossible that it became simpler for her in the end to sell the place and move out altogether.

Then their luck changed again with the promise of a great retrospective of Colquhoun's work at the Whitechapel Gallery in March 1958, on condition that he contributed several new paintings.

Colquhoun was inspired by this new incentive, and I could sense his excitement as he assured me, 'This should mean a new lease of life. It may seem a bit early to have an exhibition like this, but the moment a painter has a retrospective there's a next move forward. I want to do something that looks like something.' In a moment of rare grandiloquence, he declared, 'The canvases are going to be bigger than ever before.'

'Why are you making them so much bigger?' I asked enthusiastically.

He looked surprised. 'Because it's such a big gallery.'

For a short time the Roberts vanished from Soho. Sober and industrious, they completed the new paintings and left for a well-earned holiday. While they were away, thieves broke into their studio and stole, mutilated, or destroyed most of the pictures. Simultaneously the council announced that the property they lived in would be demolished, so the Roberts were evicted and returned to Soho and the doorsteps of pubs, waiting for them to open. Is it surprising that Colquhoun smouldered? Yet he did so with a fine anger rather than bitterness, and MacBryde retained his sense of the absurd.

The dandified writer with the silver-topped cane, Julian Maclaren Ross, who was another regular at the Caves, tried to annoy him by asking, 'What do you think about when you're sober? Do you prepare apologies for the people you've been rude to?'

MacBryde thought this over. 'Mebbe I'm thinking up new rude things to say next time I'm drunk.'

The two Roberts were casualties of Soho. Several women found Colquhoun irresistible, for of the two he seemed to need mothering the most and neither his rudeness nor his proclaimed homosexuality made the slightest difference. If anything, it added to his attraction. 'Spinster girls nearly swooned at sight of his aesthetic mouth,' wrote Maclaren Ross, 'so masterful and clamped determinedly tight, as one of them described it longingly to me.' Ross concluded that the girls of Soho were 'always subconsciously eager to break something up'.

I realise now that they were a fine couple and it gave me pleasure to see one of Robert Colquhoun's large canvases looming impressively in the Scottish Museum of Modern Art in Edinburgh. Unlike most of his contemporaries, he never taught but he gave this advice, which serves as a sort of epitaph: 'Make it with love and keep it simple.' Students quoted this so often that Rodrigo Moynihan at the Royal College of Art could stand it no longer and urged them to 'Make it with hate and keep it complicated.'

Colquhoun died in the arms of MacBryde in 1962. The lone Robert moved to Dublin, where he met his own death four years later, struck by a car as he staggered back from the pubs.

5.30 p.m. The Afternoon Fades

Such boisterous spirits had to wilt and began to do so at 5.30 p.m. when the Caves assumed a new and slightly suburban identity, as three middle-aged men stepped on to the tiny platform beside the rows of wine barrels and started to tune their instruments with the solemnity of a string quartet. They wore evening dress with white shirts and ready-made bow ties. One sported a jet black toupée which deceived nobody, while the drummer had a pronounced limp. The leader of the group was a dignified personality with a grey, military moustache, who attached a cumbersome contraption to the piano – usually at the mercy of one-fingered drunks – which transformed it miraculously into an electric organ. Once they were ready, the organist, violinist and drummer launched into a sequence of genteel dance numbers which struck me as preposterous in such distraught surroundings until I grew accustomed to the paradox and it became the norm. While a number of the Bohemian regulars remained, a new contingent arrived who looked ordinary by comparison until I realised that they were nearly as drunk as the 'afternoon men'.

One couple came every Friday and Saturday and sat on the edge of the platform, swaying in a blissful state of stupor. The man, with a neat moustache and balding scalp like the bureaucrat in an Ealing comedy, moving his hands with serpentine gestures, raising them slowly above his head as if he were a Javanese dancer performing the rope-trick, though strictly sedentary. His eyes were usually half-closed in concentration.

In contrast, the woman was Amazonian with gigantic hands and feet and a fat, flushed face. Sitting beside the man she danced with her torso, leaning backwards until she almost fell over, recovering her balance with a plunge forward, swaying against the rhythm with a grimace that suggested considerable pain, though it must have been a form of pleasure. I never saw them speak to anyone and imagined that they were in the throes of an illicit love affair, escaping from the tedium of their conventional families. One Friday they failed to appear and I was so concerned that I greeted them when they turned up on the Saturday and even had a few words of conversation. They proved extrordinarily dull, and seldom spoke because they had little to say. And, of course, they were wholly respectable, a husband and wife from the suburbs.

Deakin turned the transformation of the Caves to his advantage. Assuming a new role of Master of Ceremonies, twirling an imaginary moustache, he jumped on to the stage and introduced the daughter of the French owner with a leer worthy of the compère in *Cabaret*. The club-owner's daughter was a plump, constantly smiling, middle-aged lady named Hortense and he resorted to a series of grimaces and sarcasms which she accepted as graciously as if they were bouquets presented to a *diva*.

'And now,' he proclaimed, asking for a roll on the drums, 'let me present the girl' – he eyed her up and down incredulously – 'the *girl* you have all been waiting for so impatiently. She possesses the most incomparable voice in the world – what you have done to deserve this I cannot imagine.' He bowed to the few who were paying attention and she started to sing light opera with a fluttering of eyelashes. At first he watched enthralled, raising his spaniel eyes to heaven as she trilled archly up and down the scales. Then, in a deafening whisper he said to me, 'Come on, kiddo, let's get the hell out of here.'

'Why don't you fuck off?' cried Robert Colquhoun as we left.

Sinning in Soho

There was more fun in five minutes in the Caves de France than an evening of sin in Soho. The district's reputation for villainy and vice was manufactured largely by imaginative journalists in bars far outside the district. 'The square mile of vice' was an easy label, used by two Sunday columnists in particular who delighted in giving Soho a bad name by presenting a scene of exaggerated violence with drug addicts, gambling dens, razor slashing, wide boys, and unspeakable sex. Their stories would start along these lines: 'As I walked along one of Soho's murky backstreets, a sinister figure stepped out of a doorway. It was Scarface, the nark. " 'Ere,' he said in a hoarse whisper . . .'

Yet it was possible to walk through Soho at night and see nothing more shocking than the usual fight at closing time and the usual prostitutes. The streets of Soho were lined with them, many earning more than £20 a night which was a considerable sum of money for those days. Their rents were high and at one shop a van drew up every evening with mattresses for the girls, removing them in the morning when the establishment resumed its respectable business.

James Keely, a fishmonger in Berwick Street market for the last fifty-seven years, told me, 'I would not live here rent-free. The place is foul, polluted. It's not nice to bring a respectable lady here at night. Every other house is a brothel with tarts stopping you at the corner to ask "Do you want a strong woman for the night?" I ask you.' He snorted with indignation. But his reaction was the exception. Most of the shopkeepers did not find the prostitutes a nuisance and said that they paid their debts more quickly than anyone else. If they drank in a pub they tried to be inconspicuous, so when Marie ran into the French to escape a policeman, two of her colleagues drove her out again.

As for the soliciting, I found it hugely flattering the first time it happened, and when this wore off I still acknowledged their greetings cheerfully as I grew to know them.

The girls in Soho were better natured than those in the neon-lit streets of Piccadilly and Leicester Square, who were so brazen that they once attacked the wife of an American officer because they resented her appearance on their 'beat'.

Kindness should not be examined too closely for the motive, but deserters from the armed forces told tales of the tarts' generosity and there seemed to be an innate loyalty to the pimps, as well as fear. One man beat up a girl so often and so brutally that he was sent to prison and she was urged never to see him again. The moment he was released, she was waiting and when I knew her she sent her earnings to him in the country where he had retired while she paraded down Brewer Street, older, iller and slightly hysterical.

The turnover from one room amazed me, with men coming in and out with the regularity of a conveyor belt, and I was surprised to learn that one of the most successful girls was a lesbian, keeping a girl friend in her turn. You could find most of the vices in Soho if you looked hard enough and were ready to pay. I heard that there were pornographic films (legalised later in a membership cinema) and 'exhibitions'.

As for crime, Soho's reputation was worse than the reality. In the thirties there had been a series of unsolved murders which gave rise to the scare of a new Jack the Ripper: French Fifi was strangled in a Soho flat in 1935; Jeanette Cotton was strangled with a silk scarf in 1936; Constance Hind was battered with a flat iron, a thin wire around her neck; French Marie was strangled in a blazing flat in 1937. It was ironic that so many of the girls thought that a French prefix was as useful as a French letter.

Largely due to the big clean-up ordered by Detective Superintendent Sparks, there were few cases of robbery or assault in the fifties. Jack Spot and Billy Hill were both called 'King of Soho' but this was a label they applied to themselves. Another petty villain was Italian Albert Dimes. One morning in bright sunlight, Spot and Dimes ran into each other in Old Compton Street. After a cry of 'You've been asking for this for a long time!' passers-by saw a stiletto flash in the air as the blade plunged into Spot's flesh. The two men struggled with each other until they fell into the continental grocers on the corner of Frith where Madame hit them over the head with a heavy pair of scales. Fleeing from her violence, Spot staggered into a barber shop while Italian Albert collapsed in a taxi. The police visited both men, who recovered in hospital, but no charges were made. Everyone enjoyed the flurry, especially the Fleet Street columnists who headlined a front-page report on 'Soho Gang Warfare', claiming that a criminal just released from prison had formed an East End gang which had encroached on Jack Spot's territory and threatened his hold over the street-bookies. More likely, it was a personal vendetta with an accidental element of *opéra bouffe*.

Billy Hill was more sinister, seldom seen because he spent much of his time on board ship being refused admittance to the countries where he wished to settle. Nicholas Bentley, a partner of the publisher André Deutsch, arranged that someone from Scotland Yard should escort me around Soho's more villainous haunts one evening. The unfortunate policeman, who did not relish this assignment, took me to a club run by Billy Hill's wife, where I was introduced to Billy Hill himself. I decided that his unpleasant reputation was confirmed by his face, which had the sallow complexion of underdone pork; his eyes were piggy too.

Soho's sin was that of promise rather than reality, exemplified by the adverts in the newsagent's windows, though these struck me as surprisingly direct when I learned to read between the lines. Many dealt with 'corporal punishment', and one was signed with an address: 'Dear Madam or Sir, If you are interested in the art of corporal punishment in all its varied aspects I would very much like to hear from you, correspond with you, and later meet you, as I am a young bachelor, thirty-four years old, of similar taste and disposition. Should a lady see this "humble" notice, her letter would be doubly welcome.'

Other cards were varied though sometimes veiled:

Do you seek that certain someone?
Model aged nineteen free to accept bookings.
Visit Professor Cash Cooper's tattooing studios.
Kiki corsets – for either sex, my speciality tiny waists.
Lovely blond model aged nineteen. Now available for artists and photographers.
Private lessons in French.
Beauty treatment, slimming by Italian lady. [This made a change from the usual French.]
Advertiser interested in lingerie would like to hear from others.
Bacchante – let's meet some time.
'Masked girl attacks woman.' Do these headlines scare you? Take a course in self-confidence.

There was one which struck a poignant note of genuine affection: 'Dear Hilda, You and me were pals for four years and there was only a small quarrell. You took it to serious and it makes me ill thinking about you you know that we could be happy and you and me make a home and it is still waiting for you nobody is taken your place I wish you will come back to me.'

6.30 p.m. No Sunset for Soho

Like the smile on the chorus girl's face which switches off the moment she reaches the wings, Deakin crumpled the moment he stepped outside the Caves and left without a parting word.

There is a witching hour in the Mediterranean when the sun slides down the mountains, replaced by a firework display in a sky of changing colours. The local people promenade, for this is the most rewarding moment of the day. There was no sunset in Soho, but a sagging hour soon after six when spirits flagged, with the pubs half empty as they waited for the evening audience to arrive.

Then, like an orchestra, Soho started to tune up. Shrill cries and a clattering of castanets came from the flamenco dancer at the Casa Pepé, where Pepé Solsona squirted a jet of wine from a leather pouch on to his forehead, which trickled down his nose into his mouth. Jungle drums penetrated from a cellar underneath the site of St Anne's, filtering through a grille where passers-by crouched to catch a glimpse of the dancers below. An accordionist started to tour the tables in the Café Bleu, a zither player from the Tyrol. From the upstairs windows of sophisticated clubs came the sounds of a tinkling piano and the lyrics of Cole Porter:

> The faint aroma of performing seals,
> The double-crossing of a pair of heels,
> I wish I were in love again.

The most stylish of these entertainers was Mike Mackenzie at the Colony. A handsome, smiling black man, Mike manoeuvred those disgraceful stairs with difficulty, for he walked with the help of two steel sticks, but once he was behind the battered upright piano his talent was gigantic both as a composer as well as performer. His welcome was unfailing. When you opened the door in the evening, his was the first friendly face you saw, beaming with apparent pleasure as he played your favourite tune; he was Soho's equivalent of Sam in *Casablanca*. In my case he greeted me with the first song composed by Rogers and Hart – 'Wait Till You See Her' – which he introduced me to one evening after he played 'Manhattan', their last collaboration. The early song has a gentler simplicity which makes it the more delightful to me. Always unruffled and courteous, in spite of the frenzy which sometimes raged around him, Mike was popular with everyone, so it was inevitable that he should move to a grander 'venue' as he eventually did, to the Savoy. No one really replaced him but one of his longer-lasting successors was a young man called Adam who stopped at the Colony one evening on his way to an all-night film with some friends, and stayed. He was twenty years old.

Nobody was at the piano and somehow, through a barrage of insults from Madam, I sat down and played. I thought it was like a funny pub. Evidently Muriel was desperate for she came over and thrust her half-full glass of champagne covered with lipstick into my hand. Of course I stood up and she said, 'Put your bum down, Miss, and be my pianist from Monday, nine o'clock.' I didn't really have much chance, did I?

For the first three months I hardly dared to move. Not even to have a pee. I couldn't believe that just because four-letter words were used instead of punctuation, that almost everyone was fantastically friendly and ready to put up with my noise.

After several months, when he was more at ease, he began to absorb the scene:

I'm not a witty person, but I do watch things and almost all my humour is vicarious. I'm amused by someone who asks for a tune, which I never know anyhow, who is invariably the same person through forgetfulness or drink who asks for the same tune not only every time he's there, but roughly once every five minutes. I love Muriel saying 'Hello, me old mate!' to someone who's just come through the door, and then, while the guest is still being signed in, turning to Ian and whispering all too audibly: 'What the fuck's her name? Is she a member?' Often, she'll smile weakly at the person, eyeing them up and down, trying to find some bit of their anatomy that could possibly refresh her memory. As a last resort, she'll say 'Do I know you?' or 'Ian, look who it is! It's old . . .' until the memory blank is filled. But with people she knows, and there must be thousands of them, you always know where you are. No beating about the bush; you're either a good mate or you're not. I do wish that some people who are quite obviously *not* would realise sooner. I get so embarrassed when someone goes through those well-known rites of sacrifice. Self-sacrifice rather. There is no excuse for overstaying a patently wilting welcome.

Queer Goings-on

Some of the risqué lyrics which drifted down from an upstairs room in the early evening or permeated faintly from a shuttered basement came from clubs which were used by homosexuals. In France or America their equivalent might have been extravagant but in London the 'queer' clubs were slightly shabby in the literal sense of the word, and slightly glum. Most were well run with little to differentiate them at a first glance from the so-called 'normal' clubs. A closer look revealed the bright, watching eyes and the casual remark which led carefully into conversation.

The worst thing about such clubs was their ennui, an apathy of film extras waiting for the director to appear and call out 'Action!' True to Soho where people were constantly searching for something or someone, the young men who came to the 'queer' clubs were desperately in need of entertainment to alleviate the tedium of their lives. The queens helped to provide the distraction.

There were many bitchy young queens but the true queen was a grander species altogether, visiting the 'queer' clubs as an antidote to his daily respectability. The rules were as clearly defined as the rules of other male bastions such as Boodle's or White's, though the game was different. One club shocked me, but that was only at first, because it provided a meeting place for very young men, some of them boys under the age of eighteen and men who were considerably older, if not aged. On nights of fancy-dress balls, this small club became a scene of travesty as men paused on their way to a party dressed in wigs, fish-net stockings, evening dress, or costumes of indeterminate sex, tight-fitting and black with coloured hands sewn on to strategic places. Some carried this off with hysterical panache, others looked uneasy and ridiculous. I made a note at the time – for I scribbled copiously about my days and nights in Soho when it was all discovery – that 'the wild abandon which these people enjoy on such rare evenings of outlet is rather pathetic. British law has succeeded in making homosexuality either listlessly respectable, or simply embarrassing when it asserts itself.'

'*These people.*' How patronising! Yet the point was valid, for homosexuality was against the law, which meant that everyone who visited a 'queer' club did so with the constant threat of imprisonment. A few had been sent to prison. Most knew of a friend caught up in a sudden purge in the provinces due to the vigilance of the local police where men like Rupert Croft Cooke served their sentences and left for a self-imposed exile in a place where such behaviour was tolerated, preferably Tangier.

The owner of the 'queer' club placed himself at risk. Far from being a furtive sort of person he was usually an upright gentleman, middle-aged and enthusiastic, neatly dressed, though an inspection might reveal the frayed collars of a country squire or a retired military man. Frequently, the owner *had* been a major or a naval commander and sported a tie to that effect, or at least a tie which signified something, if only a minor public school. The war had given him the happiest years of his life, for he had responded with bravery leading his men across the lines, an exercise which accounted for the occasional limp or gammy arm. The scar on the forehead was more recent and less honourable, due to a bit of trouble late one night in the club, and not discussed.

For some reason a club-owner was known by his full name – Leonard Lane, Bobby Fortescue, Billy Wilton, to mention a few,

while his female counterpart was known invariably by her first –
Muriel, Dolly, and Dot.

The club-owner erected a façade. Usually an alcoholic – a
penalty of the environment – he took pains to appear immaculate
on the morning after with only a few tell-tale signs, such as the
watery eyes which he dabbed with the silk handkerchief thrust into
his sleeve. He had impeccable manners and greeted his members
like the Duke of Beaufort welcoming the Queen to Badminton. He
had travelled extensively – everything was in the past tense – and
knew a number of celebrities, especially Noël, of whom he was
fearfully fond in spite of the scabrous stories he recounted. He
adored women and greeted them effusively. Indeed, his liking for
women was more genuine than that of the womaniser. He had been
married himself, a brief detour, a well-known secret which
impressed the younger members considerably, like grief. It
confirmed their opinion that he was all right. And so he was. Apart
from that unfortunate marriage, his homosexuality was a fact of
life, something to be neither proud of nor ashamed of, just the
throw of the dice to be accepted with the brightest of smiles. In
different circumstances he would have been reputable; as the
owner of a 'queer' club he was beyond the pale because such
practices were criminal. In spite of the pressures, he managed to
remain 'gay' in the old sense of that ill-treated word.

7.30 p.m. Just a Little Jazz

'The great thing about jazz,' wrote Colin MacInnes, 'is that no
one, not a soul, cares what your class is, what your race is, what
your income is, or if you're a boy or a girl or bent or versatile or
what you are.' This meant a lot in the fifties.

At 7.30 p.m. at 100 Oxford Street, the doors opened into a large,
ugly, smoke-filled basement where dancers twisted and turned to
Humphrey Lyttleton's London Jazz Club band with a frenzied
discipline, until they were joined by Humph's ex-Etonian friends

who jitterbugged and jived with the total lack of rhythm of the English upper classes, grinning fatuously as they galumphed and collided with flailing arms.

The atmosphere was that of uninhibited enjoyment, an ecstasy of dripping faces and distorted bodies reaching a climax with the final scream from the trumpet as 'Bunny Bum' Melly sank to the floor with his final chorus of 'Frankie and Johnny'.

No alcoholic drinks were served – 'temples devoted to cold coffee and hot sex', as I believe John Mortimer called them –but the proximity of the sweaty bodies, with partners sometimes left bereft as the other went off to be sick or with someone else, offered frequent success if you were trying to pick someone up.

In total contrast, Colin MacInnes took me to the Abalabi, where a coloured man and a white girl danced with apparent indifference, seldom touching, their eyes ignorant of each other's existence, even turning their backs as if to avoid a confrontation, until the drums began to beat out a calypso rhythm rising to greater intensity as it took possession and the small room was filled with close pulsating bodies – yet the faces remained passive and the eyes half-dead.

8.00 p.m. The 'Queer Pubs'

The Golden Lion

In Soho there were two 'queer pubs' as they were called then: the Fitzroy off Charlotte Street to the north, and the Golden Lion in Dean Street. Though the Lion was a few doors away from the French, the two pubs had so little in common that they might have been in separate towns. Married couples wandered into the Lion by mistake and left swiftly when they discovered that they were surrounded by strange men, or remained, delighted by their chance discovery; but Gaston did not encourage stragglers who crossed the frontier for a change of scene, and one of his quizzical stares sufficed to scare them off again. Only a few customers were regulars of both: Deakin in particular.

The Golden Lion was a regular port of call on Deakin's daily meanderings through Soho. One morning he ordered a white wine and was so impatient for his first drink of the day that he swallowed most of it in a single gulp and fell to the floor gasping for breath. The barman had filled an empty bottle with Parazone, a particularly violent bleach, and poured this out by mistake. Perhaps his throat was immune to the fiery liquids poured down it over the years, but Deakin did not seem as ill as he should have been when he tottered into the French pub, exuding sickly, hygienic fumes. I made an appointment with my doctor, pointing out that if he was going to sue the brewers for negligence as he intended, he would need medical evidence to support him. He returned that afternoon jauntily saying that he had coughed up spots of blood, failing to add as the doctor explained to me later that these were the dregs of the red wine he had consumed at lunchtime. In due course Deakin did receive his damages though he never revealed how much, yet he remained on friendly terms with the landlady, Mrs Woodall, throughout.

There were several landlords over the years and every time the Lion was taken over it was 'done up' yet re-emerged with the same atmosphere as before, even when it was transformed into a medieval dungeon, with exactly the same customers. Among Mrs W's successors were an innocent young couple, newly wed from Scotland, who achieved their life's ambition by managing a pub in the heart of London. They had been in the Lion once before on a rapid tour of inspection with the area manager and had failed to notice anything unusual. On the morning of the change-over, as accountants sat at a corner-table comparing invoices and stock, the previous tenants wished them 'good luck' with such sly smiles that a less innocent couple might have been alarmed. Instead they accepted the good wishes and stood behind their bar, greeting the first customers of the day effusively, until it dawned on them slowly that all these customers were men. And some were rather odd men at that. At first they were shaken by their misfortune, then they decided to accept it; and after a few days they were on first-name terms with the regulars and became fiercely protective. When the husband ran off with the barmaid who served in the smaller, posher bar upstairs, it was the turn of the regulars to look after the landlady who insisted on staying on, despite the protests of the brewer. She was a cheerful, red-haired girl and when she returned to Scotland a year or two later she missed the Lion so much that she came back every few months to keep in touch with the friends she had made there. In some respects the Lion resembled the happy bordello of a Hollywood musical.

Customers headed for the Lion on a Friday night to pick up the servicemen who headed there for weekend leave. Far from being furtive, the exchanges were open. The only trouble came at closing time if someone saw his prey go off with another civilian who looked richer and less outrageous than himself. Sailors were the elite; guardsmen were less popular because they were known to be out for money and frequently became difficult, if only to justify their actions to themselves. Guardsmen had their barracks nearby which they could return to, but sailors travelled from Chatham, Portsmouth or distant naval ports like Plymouth, and needed somewhere to stay, so it made sense to do so at someone else's expense rather than pay for a night's kip at the Union Jack Club or suffer on a bench at Waterloo Station. This helped to provide an alibi, if an alibi were needed, for the proverbial 'good run ashore'. Incredible though it seems today, such 'goings-on' were part of the naval tradition which included 'drink, sodomy and the lash', so the sailors who came to the Lion did so with neither guilt nor shame, which was why the pub had such a jolly atmosphere. Friendships often continued after the sailor was demobbed, even surviving marriage when the 'friend' might well be a guest at the wedding, and the wives were either too naïve or too wise to question the 'friendship'.

It might be wondered why homosexuals went in pursuit of 'trade' when there were plenty of young men of their own kind who

were available. But in those days they went to the Lion because
they did not want their own kind. Their guilt at being homosexual
was lessened by making friends with men from a different
background, to whom they could offer a good time as well as the
'fare home', or whatever euphemism was used for the money which
was given as a parting gift. Homosexuals who needed to live a lie
during office hours could relax in the company of strangers in the
Lion, and be themselves, using the bar as a stage for their
extravagance. Sailors had another overwhelming advantage: there
was no danger of them lingering beyond their weekend leave.
When asked why she liked sailors so much Nina Hamnett replied:
'Because they go away.'

The Fitzroy

On the northern side of Oxford Street, Soho's other 'queer' pub,
the Fitzroy, was scandalous by comparison with the Golden Lion.
It was known as the Fitzroy 'Tavern' and for once this swash-
buckling term was apt. As the heart of Fitzrovia, the Fitzroy had
been the watering-hole for such carefully rehearsed Bohemians as
Augustus John, whose promiscuity was so legendary that it was
said that he patted the head of every child he passed in Charlotte
Street in case it was one of his. Apart from Augustus John and Nina
Hamnett, who reigned as dissolute royalty, the Fitzroy had been a
meeting place for artists of a previous generation when it was run
by a Russian known as Papa Kleinfeld. 'If I knew the Yiddisher for
"gentleman",' wrote John, 'I would use it to describe Mr
Kleinfeld.' Following the example of Constable, one of the earliest
and most distinguished residents of Fitzroy Street, numerous
artists had moved there in the thirties, including Walter Sickert,
Roger Fry, Duncan Grant, Matthew Smith and Rex Whistler.
Later it became more literary, used by Dylan Thomas, Stephen
Spender and Louis MacNeice. Like the French, the Fitzroy
catered for a close-knit community, well described by the poet
John Heath-Stubbs: 'For many people it was in a real sense their

home . . . the only place where they really related to other people. It was a very definite society with its own curious codes, its own hierarchy. Nina stood high in that hierarchy in terms of a kind of respect. She was always there every night and one always treated her with politeness, bought her a drink, listened to her stories.' Augustus John compared the Fitzroy to Clapham Junction on the grounds that sooner or later everyone had to pass through it.

When I arrived, welcoming a change of scene in the early evening, there was a sense of *déjà vu* – everything had gone before. At that hour the Fitzroy was usually deserted, apart from such ghosts as Sylvia Gough who belonged to the past. An acknowledged rival of Nina, though they barely spoke to each other, Sylvia had been a celebrity too, a famous beauty, the proverbial 'toast of London society', and a model for Sargent, Orpen and John, who was cited in one of her divorces. Compared to Nina's promiscuity which was positively off-hand – 'Can't see anything in it myself . . . But they seem to like it so I let them get on with it' – Sylvia's fondness for young men appeared more desperate. In 1936, she appeared at the Fitzroy with a black eye after she was beaten up by the 21-year-old writer she was living with, called Douglas Michael Bose. Douglas Burton, described by Denise Hooker in her biography of Nina Hamnett as 'obviously unbalanced and made self-conscious by a facial disfigurement', took pity on Sylvia Gough and took her home, looking after her for the next few days until they went to a party where Bose appeared. Burton attacked him with a sculptor's hammer, and killed him. After this 'singularly squalid and unpleasant case' the judge found Burton guilty but insane.

Soho imparts a moral story, for the pleasure-seekers invariably paid for their fun. Nina had been a celebrity in Paris; Sylvia Gough had danced in the Ziegfeld Follies in New York. Surviving on a tiny allowance, Sylvia had become a near-destitute Fitzrovian drunk, passively sitting there alone in the early evening, but she possessed a gallant perseverance going to the public baths every day to keep clean. She was so emaciated that her skin was translucent, revealing her skeletal bones, yet she remained charming, courteous and grateful for company. I never heard a bad word said against her. Bruce Bernard remembers her as 'just one of the loveliest ladies ever'. In that early evening there was so little hint of the riot to come that when an American couple stopped me in the street to ask for a 'typically English pub', I sent them to the Fitzroy to see the splendid recruiting posters of the First World War which decorated the walls, and the framed telegrams sent by Queen Mary, which thanked the publican, Charlie Allchild, who had married Kleinfeld's daughter, for the contributions to her charities such as the annual outing of local poor children to the seaside. These donations were wrapped in silver paper and attached to the ceiling, where they were thrown with darts and hung like tiny stalactites. I thought that the nice American couple would approve of such a patriotic atmosphere and was appalled when I heard that the Fitzroy had been raided by the police later that night.

If the Lion was a marketplace, the Fitzroy came closer to an Eastern bazaar after nine o'clock when it was so crowded that it was difficult to move. A bearded man in a kilt played the piano and there was a constant procession to the Gents downstairs with a gauntlet of penetrating stares on the way. As the evening developed, the atmosphere was one of frenzied celebration and the sailors misbehaved as if they were on leave in Port Said surrounded by houris, as to a certain exent they were in the eyes of the visiting Metropolitan Police.

Describing the Fitzroy as a 'den of vice', the police counsel stated:

> For the most part its occupants were quite obvious male homosexuals who dyed their hair and rouged their cheeks and behaved in an effeminate manner with effeminate voices. The other occupants were to a very large extent made up of servicemen – sailors, soldiers and marines. There can be very little doubt that this house was conducted in a most disorderly and disgusting fashion. These perverts were simply overrunning the place, behaving in a scandalous manner and attempting to seduce the members of the forces.

The police also charged that the Fitzroy was the habitual resort of reported prostitutes, but on the night of this raid it was pointed out to the publican that (apart from the American couple if they had lingered) eighty of the men present were perverts.

'I didn't think it was as bad as that,' said Charlie.

Not a man to be browbeaten, Charlie Allchild refuted the charges vigorously but the brewers, with their customary cowardice, suspended him during the hearings. To their astonishment he was acquitted of all the charges which were wilfully extravagant and welcomed him back in triumph, for their profits had been immense. But Charlie had too much pride, removed his valuable collection of posters from the walls, and left. The Fitzroy has never recovered.

9.00 p.m. One More for the Road

Poetic Public Houses

If the Fitzroy was hysterically camp, other pubs in north Soho tended to be frighteningly earnest with an aggressive crowd of penniless poets and writers; including personalities like Tambimuttu, the Singalese editor of *Poetry London*, who warned Maclaren Ross: 'It's a dangerous place . . . if you get Sohoitis . . . you will stay there always day and night and get no work done ever.'

Yet these pubs were the truest to the Bohemian nature of Soho: the Duke of York, the Black Horse, and the Wheatsheaf, all crowded with people arguing until they closed at 10.30 p.m. when there was a final surge of panic across Oxford Street to the pubs further south. The discrepancy of the extra half-hour's drinking time proved once again the insanity of our licensing laws but was part of the game.

I preferred the pubs to the south of Oxford Street because this was where I started, but Bruce and Jeff Bernard used both.

Bruce and Jeffrey Bernard

Jeff had arrived in Soho before me and was equally trapped. Like a lost soul he haunted Soho, shadowed by his older brother Bruce who looked forbiddingly glum until I grew to appreciate his dry good humour. They were more experienced and 'streetwise' than me, although Jeff was five years younger.

Like many Soho drifters, the Bernard brothers – Oliver the poet, Bruce and Jeffrey – reacted against a respectable background: 'We're related to the Duke of Westminster,' Jeff claimed unconvincingly. However, they inherited an artistic flair from their mother who was an opera singer, and their father, a distinguished architect noted for his art-deco designs for the Strand Palace Hotel, the Dorchester and Lyons Corner Houses. When he died in 1939, leaving £2,000 and £7,000 of debts, Jeff was seven. It was during the holidays from Pangbourne Naval College that he was introduced to Soho by Bruce who was studying art at St Martin's in Charing Cross Road:

> He said come and have a cup of coffee in this marvellous place, and that was it. He fucked up my life completely. I was fourteen. Soho was a liberation after the horror of English schools with their cry of 'Don't' and the discipline of Pangbourne where the masters thrashed me. Suddenly I was surrounded by pretty girls, booze, nutcases, painters and writers. It was magic, at least it seemed so, like walking out of Belsen into Disneyland. I've been drunk ever since. Every day from then on I told my mother I was going to the science museum and took the tube instead from Holland Park to Tottenham Court Road to work for Victor Sassie in the Budapest as a part-time dish-washer in return for a cup of tea, a bun and a ten-bob note.

The rest of his day was spent exploring Soho. In those days the 'caff' was an intergral part of life and the Bernards made friends with Harry Dymond in the Swiss Café which was used by art students, who introduced them to Lucian Freud. At Tony's in Charlotte Street, Tony played cards with the chef all night, the 'caff' frequently changing hands in the process. 'People would talk

Jeff Bernard in Soho Square

The French pub in the early fifties: Gaston behind the bar, Mary serving, and Henrietta and Michael Law in the foreground with the composer Edward Williams

John Deakin seen at his most gleeful in the French pub, plainly relishing his caustic wit — at someone else's expense

A picture of Dean Street in the fifties which reveals a surprising amount of detail in retrospect, the more you look at it: the Champs Elysée high-class tailor, long since vanished, with 'élite stocking repairs' at only one shilling and sixpence per stocking; S Palmay the shoe specialist; a cluster of empty milk bottles against a shuttered window; and a typical Soho group talking on the street corner — though I had forgotten how many black people were present in those early days

Portrait of Daniel Farson by John Deakin

The artist Nina Hamnett guarded by Peter Mons Berlemont

Two sailors on leave in Soho chatting up the regulars at the Fitzroy. At first glance this picture gives the misleading impression that it was taken in the First World War. In fact the posters on the wall were part of the landlord's private collection

An inverterate gambler, Francis Bacon fronted for a club in the last war. His old nanny took the coats and hats. This rare print shows that even a slot machine was irresistible

An historic lunch at Wheeler's photographed by John Deakin. left to right Timothy Behrens, Lucian Freud, Francis Bacon, Frank Auerbach and Michael Andrews — already the most formidable painters in Britain in the fifties

Francis Bacon

Muriel Belcher on her corner-stool at the Colony Room in Dean Street, where, with uncanny instinct, she assembled a power-house of talent around her

Norman Balon, 'the rudest landlord in London'

Ian Board and Peter Bradshaw outside the Braganza in Frith Street

Jeffrey Bernard — synonymous with Soho: a man who relishes wit, good food and drink and pungent conversation, and detests bores, sham, pomposity and closing-time

philosophy all day long and borrow two shillings and sixpence at the end of it.'

Bruce says, 'I've met all the people I've ever cared about in Soho. I just hung around too long – a couple of decades too long.'

Always honest regarding himself, Jeff admits to a sense of relief on his mother's death: 'I felt slightly delighted – a *terrible* thing to say – but I felt free, no longer someone to answer to.' It could be said that he has been searching for someone to mother him ever since; several of his wives might agree.

John Minton

Jeff was sixteen when he met the painter John Minton in the Black Horse. It might be more accurate to say that the artist met Jeff, for Minton was an avid collector of young people. He taught Sandy Fawkes when she studied at the Camberwell School of Art, who says: 'He was wonderful. Like a Pied Piper he gathered us up and took us West to places like the Leicester Square Jazz Club where I met my future husband, Wally. Johnny was very much an introducer of people into Soho and when I was eighteen he bought me my first drink, a gin and orange cordial, in the French.'

Minton was brilliant but flawed. He was a fine artist, draughtsman and designer whose touch was instantly recognisable, but this was not enough. He told John Moynihan: 'After Matisse and Picasso, there is nothing more to be done,' a curious admission of defeat from someone so talented, for he was far from second-rate. Perhaps his gift was facile, making it seem too easy to himself as well as to others. When Sandy stayed the weekend at his home in Hamilton Terrace, he painted her portrait, and another of Bobby Hunt who was staying there too; he started on the Saturday, finished on Sunday, and sent off the pictures on Monday for a new exhibition.

Perhaps he was too febrile in his lust for life, hating to be alone, always moving with an entourage, swooping up to Soho in a crowded taxi from Chelsea, laughing uproariously – so much the life and soul of the party that he was in danger of killing it dead. Yet even when he led them astray, his students gained from his vitality: 'He conveyed real enthusiasm for work,' Sandy Fawkes remembers gratefully. 'You'd go home and draw until midnight.'

John Moynihan met Minton when he was teaching at the Royal College of Art Painting School where John's father, Rodrigo, was a professor: 'He evoked at once an irresistibly magical aura of ebullience and *joie de vivre* and it was not surprising that so many young people surrounded and admired him.'

I remember that when I saw him advancing, almost prancing down Dean Street, there was a sense that bells were ringing. Conversely, his long El Greco face, captured so powerfully in the portrait by Lucian Freud, would elongate even further when it was sunk in gloom. Then he would leap to his feet again.

Though consumed by his homosexuality, I doubt if that was a problem. That was one of the astonishing aspects of Soho at that time – few people were bothered. This would not have been the case in the suburbs or the provinces, where homosexuality was a stigma, but in Soho people were so preoccupied with having fun that class, age and sexual preferences were irrelevant. Minton made a mockery of being queer and behaved with an abandon which might raise eyebrows today but was welcomed as healthy exuberance then. No one could accuse Minton of the worst vice in Soho, that of being boring. In this respect Soho was a club where kindred spirits gathered by instinct, and some people could never infiltrate however long they stood at the bar and however many drinks they bought for us.

Minton's main difference was money: unlike most of us, he had lots of it. His commercial work was highly successful and it was rumoured that he had inherited a sum from Minton china. He was apt to refer to his inheritance with wild disdain – 'Let's spend it!' – though this does not mean that it actually existed. If it did exist, and whatever the source, it might have produced a guilt similar to Archer's. Significantly the two men were wary of each other, for Minton also behaved as if he had an obligation to share it. While Archer slipped the odd pound note surreptitiously, Minton brandished it, but this should not belittle his innate generosity. When John Moynihan was a steward of the Artists' Benevolent Institution, he received a contribution from Minton with the accompanying note: 'I feel most strongly that all of us who practise and derive such pleasure from the arts, have a right to ask one another for help at critical times, and the generosity of artists is something which has always kept faith with their belief in creative activity . . .'

Probably he was searching for the impossible: the perfect friend, or 'the Nietzche of the football team', as Francis Bacon called it, for most of the young men he picked up became friends rather than lovers. Bobby Hunt remembers him with such affection that he wishes they *had* slept together. 'I mean we slept in the same bed but we never had sex.' (Minton bit his fingers so savagely that the sheets were stained with his blood.)

> Now I think why on earth not, if it would have given him some pleasure?
>
> One day my father asked me, 'Who is this man gives you presents and takes you to the ballet?'
>
> 'He's my teacher,' I told him.
>
> 'Oh, I think I'd better meet him.'
>
> When I told Johnny that my dad was a huge copper he did not go for the idea at all, but of course when they did meet they got on like a house on fire!
>
> Finally my dad asked if I was a 'nance' or 'pansy', or whatever word was used then, for they were the only people I seemed to know.
>
> I told him I wasn't but I liked them – 'They've been good to me, they're the only people who've really helped me.'
>
> He thought this over and nodded: 'Well if they've helped you, you're quite right to be nice to them.'

Jeff Bernard had a similar experience with Minton: 'My mother, would you believe, thought he was a philanthropist because he gave me a daily allowance of ten shillings a day. When he took me to Spain, she thought he was after my mind and not my beautiful body!' Jeff shakes with laughter at her naïvety.

Jeff's own obsessive pursuit of girls did not deter him from accepting Minton's patronage, especially when he took Jeff to Paris and gave him the money to pay for a whore. 'Her name was Mimi,' Jeff remembers. 'I was very randy then. Bobby Hunt, Peter Dunbar and I fucked her three times a day.'

Apart from paying for their whores and buying their drinks, Minton inspired genuine devotion.

'One of the best people, Johnny,' said Henrietta, who was closer to him than most. 'Very rare indeed, and so *witty*! He liked brave boys basically, and I'm brave, aren't I? *Aren't I?*'

'Were you in love with him?'

'But of course.'

In Johnny's tortuous way, he was in love with her. It seemed that everyone loved him and everyone loved her. Then the predictable occurred – Johnny found the ideal young man he had been looking for: attractive, original, strong, whose good humour made him popular with everyone; and in due course this Adonis fell in love with Henrietta. One day Minton made the mistake of telling him, 'You must choose between us.'

'My heart fell to my boots,' says Henrietta, 'for I dreaded that he was going to choose me and he did. He was all right as a lover and I was pregnant by him, but oooh . . .' – she shook her head angrily – 'it was always *étonne moi* with Johnny, he was a really, really big presence. Why did he care so bloody much?'

I have no idea if it shattered Minton to lose them both, though Henrietta says, 'He wasn't happy, was he?' She believes that he was pursued by the idea of the law bursting in on him. 'I wanted him to tell the law what to do, but you needed super-glue to stand up to them then. Such a twerp to give in.' Maclaren Ross described him as 'torn to pieces by tiny marmosets'.

Minton's lodger told me later of the night in 1957 when Minton's newest friend phoned from a party to say that he might be staying the night there. The lodger tip-toed into Johnny's bedroom and reported that he was fast asleep. The friend phoned again in the morning and this time the lodger reported that Minton was 'still sleeping it off', so the friend stayed on for lunch. By the time he returned in the late afternoon, it was too late. Minton had taken a massive overdose. The lodger believed that it was done to stage a reconciliation scene when the friend arrived in time to save him, but, if so, it all went wrong. It was such a waste.

Minton, who had been so kind, had the last vengeful laugh: he left his splendid Chelsea home to Henrietta; the young man whom he loved, but who had chosen her, got nothing.

10.00 p.m. The Night Wears On

The sad violinist played in the doorway of the alley which connected Rupert and Berwick Street markets; nearby, a sterner-faced man shouted religion as he handed tracts to the passers-by, who dropped them in the gutter where they lay accusingly, threatening doom and destruction among the wood shavings and the rotten apples.

A very old man with a deeply lined face toured the pubs with a tray of delicate violets. In the French, someone bought the entire contents and distributed the flowers to all the ladies present. I looked across, for I thought the old man would be overjoyed, but utter dejection showed instead – the justification of his day was over.

Another man with a tray edged up behind me disconcertingly, murmuring, 'Any health mags, love stories?' producing a few frayed health magazines catering for nudists and physique enthusiasts. With his sinister bi-focals and peaked cap, he qualified as one of the first Soho purveyors of porn, but it was soft stuff indeed and I never saw him make a sale.

The jolly newspaper-seller had done his evening round and was having a beer. As he was illiterate, he settled for the constant cry of 'Nearly annuver murder!' which was fair enough until the day he stopped a couple of passers-by to ask what the headlines *really* said and astonished everyone by continuing up the street shouting, 'Hitler found in Camden Town!'

Eating Late

For most people, Soho came into its own in the evening, due to the rich variety of restaurants which gave the district its repuation for good living.

Gennaro's was the oldest Italian restaurant in Soho with only one customer when it opened at 44 Dean Street and as many as 1,200 on a single day since, including Melba and Caruso and the Kings of Greece, Yugoslavia and Siam. When he worked in the Cecil Hotel in 1898, Signor Gennaro waited on Edward VII (then Prince of Wales) and now he still greeted the ladies at the door of his restaurant with 'a smile and a flower' and worked ten hours a day. He told me the secret of his longevity: 'I put two pounds of washing soda in my bath for the last thirty-eight years. It keeps me so fit, I never feel I have a body. I always feel like a baby.' By now, both the restaurant and the owner where starting to show their age, the washing soda notwithstanding.

At Leoni's Quo Vadis, on the other side of the Colony at 26 Dean Street, Leoni took the orders himsef, working a fifteen-hour day which started at 5.00 a.m. when he went to Smithfield market to buy the meat and then to Covent Garden for the vegetables. The restaurant had three floors but when he started it in 1926 there was only the single room, now used as a cocktail bar and permanently occupied by a self-appointed public relations man called Lieutenant-Colonel Santos Cassani, who waxed even more lyrical than Max Beerbohm, whose declaration – 'Oh to be in London, now that Leoni's there!' –hung behind him.

'At Leoni's you are always cordially welcome and assured of Leoni's personal attention,' the Colonel informed me when I paused for a drink. 'This is my happy experience for the last twenty-three years.' He screwed a monocle into his eye and pointed triumphantly to a far corner. 'Look!' he exclaimed. 'A man sitting by himself and a woman sitting by herself. Will she look at him? Certainly not!'

I shook my head in agreement.

'And will he speak to her? Never, not even if she is the most beautiful woman in the world, and she is *not*! They have come here to *eat*! I'm probably old enough to be your grandfather so you may not know who I am. There's talk of a film of my life, you know I was blinded in the First World War, and I am writing my story *Not Conquered*. In the last war I was seconded to the Indian Army in Burma and if it had not been for Independence I might have made a great deal of money and received a knighthood. Instead I ran the Cassani nightclub and the Cassani school for dancing, which you know of, of course. I am expert on beauty, physical culture, deportment and famous for success in restoring use of limbs. My wife has lost her own leg.'

To my horror I found myself smiling, thinking it might be hard to lose someone else's leg, but he broke off to point to Mr Leoni who was looking across sympathetically as if I might be in need of help.

'I ask Leoni,' said the Colonel, 'when you retire? "Never," he says. 'This is not my work, it is my pleasure." '

Leoni overheard and beamed at me. I beamed back. The Colonel bowed, and I moved on.

Gennaro's and Leoni's are among the grandest of the old-established Soho restaurants, but there were many to choose from to suit your taste and pocket: the Budapest in Greek Street with the incomparable Victor Sassie; Madame Maurer's near Foyle's, with huge slices of delicious cake at student prices; Fava's in Frith Street where I ate superb steak with Gavin Lambert and Lindsay Anderson and when we discovered it was horse it was too late to matter; risotto at Bianchi's (Greek Street); mackerel at L'Escargot (Greek Street) where the charming old waiters wore evening dress and whose hands trembled so violently that it was rash to order soup; Au Jardin des Gourmets (Greek Street), for classic French food; and Kettner's in Romilly Street, founded in 1858, where Oscar feasted with panthers in an upstairs room.

Ironfoot Jack

Amongst the resaurants there was even the odd aberration like the short-lived restaurant run by Ironfoot Jack. In a district where so many strove to be characters, he tried too hard. A man of many professions – phrenologist, antique dealer and bookseller – his name was due to the iron frame which made up for the shortage of six inches in his left leg. He enhanced this defect by making his appearance even more bizarre with colourful silk scarves which were pinned together with an old cameo which he tried to sell whenever an unsuspecting stranger was persuaded to admire it. The effect was completed with an opera cloak and a silver-knobbed cane.

Ironfoot Jack told me that when he found some cheap, almost derelict premises in Greek Street, he became a restaurateur. The electricity was cut off so, in Fagin's wake, he persuaded his 'boys' to filch some paraffin lamps from the nearest night watchman's hut which gave the restaurant an interesting atmosphere. When a customer arrived, he flourished an enormous menu in French with all the dishes crossed out except for 'poisson et pommes frites', and if anyone commented on such a strange discrepancy he explained that this was due to a sick chef, though he eulogised about the 'poisson'. When this was ordered, he shouted to a non-existent kitchen at the back where a boy waited until he heard the cry and sprinted up the road to the nearest fish and chip shop, returning with a paper bag which was emptied on to a plate, served majestically by Ironfoot Jack himself.

The restaurant lasted for only a few weeks and he turned to fortune-telling instead.

Ironfoot Jack's determination to rise above his shortcomings was admirable, but I found him a dreadful old bore and was far from certain that his story about the restaurant was true.

11.00 p.m. Closing Time Came Too Soon

Eleven o'clock in the morning as the bolts are drawn and the pubs spring back to life is one of the blessed moments of the day, with everything to look forward to. Eleven o'clock at night is the moment of desperate truth, especially when you are young with the anguish of lost opportunities, sexual jealousy and unrequited love, all of which are cured by the light of day but seem so overwhelming then. The smoke-filled air is rent with cries of dismissal, gloating over your defeat: 'Time gentlemen please!' 'Let's be having yer' or, in the Colony, 'Back to your lonely cottages.'

In the Caves de France, Deakin went through a nightly ritual with the kind-hearted Jenny: 'Just one more, please.'

'John, we're closed. Please be a good boy and go home. We're tired. Don't you want to go to bed?'

'Why should I? There's no one else in my bed. Will you come to bed with me?'

A merry giggle at such naughtiness and a shake of the head: 'You know I can't, now do go home.'

'All right, if I can have one more drink?'

'Is that a promise?'

'Yes.'

Jenny remained doubtful. 'Really I don't know,' she hesitated, 'and there is this money you owe us.'

'I'll pay that tomorrow, Jenny.'

'That's what you said yesterday. Come on, give me that £2.' This was under the belt and Deakin slid from his stool – 'Maybe I'd better go home after all' – and staggered out. Jenny shook her head despairingly – 'and he's such a good photographer.'

With my youthful stamina, I stayed the course and looked for more. A few alternatives were left.

The Mandrake was probably the most popular of all, a downstairs club in Meard Street, opposite the Colony, where we lingered the afternoon over a cup of coffee or waited for the metal shutters to rise with a screech of relief, hoisted by the barmaid

Ruth after she unlocked the grille. Always cheerful behind her bar, Soho's version of the barmaid at the Folies Bergère, Ruth appeared in a new hair-style every day and became someone to wave to as she scooted through the streets on her Lambretta. Boris Watson, the owner, a large, unkempt man with swivelling, suspicious eyes, had started the club specifically for chess enthusiasts and could be found crouched over the board on most afternoons, but the underground atmosphere proved so popular that he began to advertise it as 'London's Only Bohemian Rendezvous'. The Mandrake continued after 11.00 p.m. with music, but I never felt wholly at ease there, suspecting that the members tried too hard to live up their Bohemian billing.

The glummest alternative of all was the clip-joint.

The Clip-joint

I was astonished that other people could be so naïve, until I remembered that I had been conned myself. In the mood for another drink, I walked towards Wardour Street when a stranger stopped me and asked, 'Are you looking for somewhere to drink?' He seemed genuinely helpful as he told me of a club which had just opened, for he didn't ask for money, nor did he stop for a drink. He left me at the foot of a dimly lit staircase where a man demanded a membership fee. I flattered myself on this 'discovery' until I reached the upstairs room and was overwhelmed by depression. The darkness did not conceal the shabbiness and through the gloom several ill-at-ease faces stared at me, recognising a fellow fool. The hostesses were pretty terrifying, instead of the other way round, greeting their victims with an insolent indifference as if we hardly mattered, nor did we to them. A smile was flashed on and off like a light-bulb and when I ordered a drink I received two electrifying shocks. First, they weren't drinks at all but a nauseating mixture of Coco Cola, ginger wine and a touch of peppermint cordial. Second the price: five shillings for ingredients which could not have cost the club more than fourpence. The hostesses received two shillings for each drink which they were bought, making yum-yum sighs of satisfaction though these were understandably half-hearted. Given a coloured cellophane disc for each glass they consumed, they cashed these in at the end of the evening.

The most astounding aspect of the clip-joint is the ease with which people are clipped. It seems that there is always a sucker in Soho, a born victim, for this practice continues up to the present day. Most of the customers write the evening off to experience, as I did, though occasionally a foreigner has the courage to complain to the police. In the fifties, when there were ten unlicensed 'near beer' clubs known to the police, a 29-year-old American student called Norman Green wandered into the Arts and Models Club in Lisle Street. The doorkeeper, a girl in a pert red uniform, led the American to a small room on the first floor with fourteen girls and a piano. As Norman neither drank nor smoked, his reason for being there was obvious, though thwarted by Sally Stevens who drank eight small cherry cocktails made from diluted blackcurrent juice, and three large ones at ten shillings each, receiving a 50 per cent commission. Norman also bought her a packet of cigarettes and gave her £6 10s. to meet him after the club closed at two o'clock in the morning, but she never appeared. When he returned to the club two days later to protest, he was given his money back but the manager, an ex-boxer, assaulted him and received two months' imprisonment.

Sally Stevens, whose real name was Angela Hopkins, was luckier. The chairman of the London Appeals Committee told her that she had been 'caught up in the toils of a frightful place. The sooner your husband shows a bit of sense and takes you away from it, the better.' As an inducement he gave her a year's conditional discharge and the couple announced their intention to emigrate.

The detective constable involved told the committee that the police tried to keep a careful watch on such clubs: 'The trouble was that the victims were most reluctant to give evidence.' And one reason for this was the publicity: bad enough to be a sucker in Soho without being laughed at in the *News of the World*.

As obnoxious as the clip-joint was the alleged 'nightclub'. After paying a membership fee, and a guest fee if accompanied, one entered an impersonal but usually empty room where the inevitable hostesses insisted on ordering a bottle of champagne which bore no resemblance to the genuine thing and so did not offend the law. Around midnight there was a roll on the drums and a cry of 'Let's get on with this wunnerful show!' whereupon two of the pluckier hostesses, tarted up with heavy make-up and short scarlet skirts, performed a song and dance with the compère clapping loudly as they left the platform: 'Thank you Bobbie and Gracie!' Then, assuming a voice more suitable for a sermon, he announced: 'And now here's a song I did last year before the King of Jamaica and also the Duke of Edinburgh.' When this tedium was over, he introduced the big climax to the show which proved to be Bobbie and Gracie all over again. The bill was the only drama and the only real surprise.

12.00 midnight Midnight Strikes

The Gargoyle

I had the luck to catch the last gasp of the Gargoyle. Next door to the Mandrake, it had known grander days. With the idea of starting a nightclub, the Hon. David Tennant bought the entire building in 1925, though it was two years before the ballroom was completed on the top floor at a total cost of £56,000.

The most astonishing aspect of the Gargoyle was the fact that the room was designed by Henri Matisse and executed by the architect Sir Edwin Lutyens. Originally it contained two magnificent Matisse murals but one was sold to America for less than £1,000 and the other was bought by Kenneth Clark for £600 and subsequently drifted to America as well. Matisse had acquired a number of mirrors which were two hundred years old, originally standing twenty-five feet high in a French château, and these were cut up into 20,000 small squares. Lutyens designed the leather curtains with an African motif. The ceiling was, or had been, covered with 22-carat gold leaf. Now it was hard to tell, and in spite of the assurance that it was still true gold above us, I had my doubts.

Courtenay Merrill, who worked in the club from the outset, retiring in the early fifties to start his own restaurant on the south coast, remembered Matisse as a boy 'who had not grown up – rather refreshing!' He was shocked by the curtains and their African motif which he considered the work of a 'fanatic'.

David Tennant and his partner, Hermione Baddeley, who became his wife, coincided with the post-war liberation of the Bright Young Things and their club was a hit from the start. The staff of fifteen grew to forty-seven and requests for membership (including my father's) at seven guineas a time poured into the committee, who rejected any application if they had the slightest doubt. From the outset, the Gargoyle was a marvellous mix of Bohemians and aristocracy: one evening there were two princes, three princesses and King Carol of Romania. In the membership book for 1926, I came across the names of Lady Horlick, the Earl of Clanwilliam, Mary Smith, and Fred and Adele Astaire. The Duke of Windsor was a regular visitor; so was Talullah Bankhead, and Brenda Dean Paul, notorious for her drug addiction, accompanied by her mother who smoked cigars seven inches long.

At the beginning the tableware was solid silver and the chef was alleged to spend an entire afternoon working on a sauce. Skirts used to be worn above the knees and people spoke to each other in French over the al fresco dinners on the roof which lasted until dawn. Evening dress was compulsory.

By the end of the thirties the party started to wind down. After the war, a new clientele drifted in, upsetting the older members with their own brand of rowdiness. This can be understood from two of the names in the membership book for 1951: Guy Burgess who joined on 8 May and Donald Maclean who signed it three days later.

In 1952, the Gargoyle was bought by John Negus whose solid appearance was misleading, for he relished the sight of his members falling apart as they tried to enjoy themselves. The Gargoyle remained exclusive, though he tried to extend the range rather than alter it, encouraging writers and artists, the penniless and the very rich. Evening dress became the pleasing exception rather than the rule, membership was only three guineas, and people wandered about as if it were a private party. Negus achieved an informal atmosphere in luxurious surroundings, for the Matisse mirrors remained surprisingly untarnished in spite of the evenings they had reflected.

The lift was the size of a telephone box, so there was usually a crowd around the entrance when the pubs closed and I rediscovered Deakin who was waiting to get inside, though David Archer was trying hard to put him in a taxi.

'Don't just stand there. Go!' Deakin shouted at him. 'Can't you see when you're not wanted?'

'Well, really,' said Archer, slipping me a flustered smile. 'I don't know. I must say. Well, if you won't, I'd better pop along.'

'Then for God's sake, *pop*! Christ how you bore the bejesus out of me.'

This was my first visit to the Gargoyle and I felt the excitement as soon as I squeezed into the lift which rose slowly to the top of the building. It was so full that when the door opened, Deakin was pushed out and fell flat on his face. 'Tanks for nuttin kid,' he sneered as I picked him up, and swayed on in. Having risen to the top, we now walked down the stairs into the large low-ceilinged room lined with the Matisse mirrors so I had the giddy sensation of being on top of the world but in the womb-like security of a basement.

This was one of the good nights, a sort of upper-class Bedlam, though the difference between the drunks and the lunatics was imperceptible. There were pockets of decorum, with Lady Diana Cooper intent at her table next to that of Johnny Minton, who was surrounded by an entourage of 'matelots'. Minton was my host and I sat at the end of the table among his rejects, while the latest favourites sat beside him. He did not have the heart to sever his relationships, so the sailors lingered on.

One reason for the vigour of the Gargoyle was the band which performed with a gaiety worthy of Joe Loss, though the leader here was a tiny man called Alec Alexander, with apparently pencilled moustache and pencilled grin as he conducted his few musicians with indefatigable zest, as if the customers were entertaining him. And, to a certain extent, this was true. Certainly he was spared the tedium of a few normal couples smooching their way gloomily around the dance floor. Instead, Johnny Minton provided a one-man cabaret as he gyrated on a dance floor the size of a tablecloth while Alec Alexander, forever dapper, played his perennial requests: 'My Very Good Friend the Milkman Said', and 'I'm Going to Sit Right Down and Write Myself a Letter', rewarded by trays of drinks which Minton sent over with his usual effusive generosity.

While Minton danced, his elongated frame dipping and darting frantically, there was scant room for anyone else. When he staggered off, Rodrigo and Eleanor Moynihan jived till the sweat poured from their faces; a large woman spun a small man as if he were a top; an old man staggered about conducting an imaginary orchestra; and an elegant couple in evening dress performed an immaculate fox-trot. Lady Diana talked on, oblivious to the commotion.

John Minton staggered back to the head of the long table, which needed to be long – several put together – because he had invited so many people, students from the art college where he taught, as well as his sailors, one of whom was eyeing a bottle suspiciously:

'What's this?'

'Champers! It's terribly good for you, dear. Much, much better than brown or mild.'

'Tastes like scrumpy,' said the sailor.

The sailors stopped talking to watch another painter who was standing on a chair eating a pound note. 'Look!' he cried, taking the pound from his wallet as if he were a conjuror. He twirled it around his head and thrust it into his mouth. I could not imagine what he was trying to prove, unless he felt eclipsed by Minton's feverish gaiety and needed an audience to impress. Instead, the sailors watched him with concern. With my awful self-righteousness I cried out 'Stop!' as he produced a beautiful, crisp five-pound note and started to stuff this into his mouth as well. This was too much for Minton who raced up and snatched the fiver, which he handed to Joe as a birthday present. Joe, a soft-voiced Scot, was the latest favourite.

'Don't be such a bloody fool,' Minton angrily told the painter, who belched loudly and ran up the stairs clutching his hand to his mouth. I felt certain that he was going to make himself sick in order to retrieve the notes from the vomit and wash them under the tap.

'Have a glass of champagne!' Minton called to me from the other end of the table, 'to celebrate Joe's birthday and spend the last fifty pounds of my inheritance.' He fussed over Joe as if he were a chorus girl, to which Joe did not object, but the other painter's exhibitionism had dampened the gaiety and soon Minton looked lugubrious, a dark melancholy clouding his face.

'He's all right,' said a former favourite next to me, 'but moody with it. Watch out.'

Minton grew sullen: 'I'm only liked because I'm rich. I can buy anyone I want.' The sailors, all of whom were in uniform, munched their steaks contentedly.

I looked around with curiosity. The atmosphere was that of a party out of control: drinks were sent generously to other tables, people wandered about casually, threw themselves into arguments and cut in on couples dancing. Lady Diana Cooper went home.

A man came over and spoke to Minton, whose face grew even longer.

'I wish you'd have a look at my things some time. I think they have something. Just jottings you know.' I gathered that the man was a poet. 'They're straight from the soul,' the man persevered desperately, receiving no reaction whatsoever, 'straight from the soul.'

'Ah, soul,' echoed Minton gloomily. Then there was an explosion of laughter – 'Arsehole!' Good humour restored, he leapt to his feet and danced a wild Charleston by himself while Alec Alexander beamed.

Suddenly, like a gramophone winding down, the gaiety ran out and the waiters bustled about with bills on plates. A hubbub of objections erupted.

'What's this?' a north-country voice demanded. 'I'm not paying any bloody ballroom fee. And what's this for sandwiches? We didn't have any bloody sandwiches.' Several people entered a back room to dispute the amount personally with Mr Negus. It was disconcerting when he chopped off large amounts as if the whole thing were a game of chance.

'Mr Deakin,' came an anguished voice, 'there's a small matter of eight shillings.'

Deakin swayed on the stairs, summoning a last vestige of dignity. 'You call yourself a headwaiter. How dare you bother me for a measly eight shillings? I'll sign for it when I come here again, *if* I come here again.' He continued up the stairs and a woman screamed as he lost his balance and almost fell backwards, but he straightened up in time and tottered on towards the lift.

'He causes more trouble than all the members put together,' sighed the waiter wearily to a couple at the next table. 'See the staff tonight? Recognise any of them? No, they all left because of Mr Deakin.'

I thought of Deakin with new admiration as I wondered how he had succeeded in running up a bill as small as eight shillings.

2.00 a.m. The Party's Over

While Minton's waving entourage drove off in a bursting taxi, I walked down Dean Street to Mrs Bill's, the coffee-stall in the bomb site by St Anne's Church, where I drank a dreadful cup of sweet coffee, eyed suspiciously by the unsuccessful flotsam of the night. It was past two o'clock in the morning.

The Soho night was nearly over. The last lift decanted the last drunk. The air was cool. Someone was sick in the gutter and I could hear the distant sound of argument. There was still that indomitable chirrup in the doorway – 'Hullo dearie!' – and then, with a final sigh, a sort of silence. Soho was a village once again.

PART TWO
ADDICTED TO SOHO

The real wickedness of Soho is subtle, it lies in the dangerous, habit-forming escape which one can find here. Perhaps nothing is so terrible as loneliness and this one could lose for a few hours at least in the kind oblivion of drink and the company of friends. Night after night one sees the same faces discussing the unfinished manuscript, the trip to be made, the picture to be painted, the dream to be fulfilled. Gradually the bad values are enhanced, there is a destructive criticism of everything and everyone, finally of one's friends and oneself. The day arrives when one must make the return to normalcy with sore mouth and sore conscience and break the dependence on Soho.

I made this entry in my diary in the fifties.

It is seldom that you learn from your own wisdom, but I have broken free from Soho on two occasions. The first time, in the mid-fifties, I was so stale from Soho that I joined the Merchant Navy and sailed round the world; yet Soho was the first destination on my return. I was addicted.

At first I was hurt that my absence had scarcely been noticed. Unlike members of one's family, no one demanded to know where I had been and what I had been doing. Such questions are considered dangerous in Soho; also, no one particularly wants to hear the answer. Instead, I was absorbed into the conversation as if I had merely gone downstairs for a pee. I was home again.

Archer's Bookshop

> Fare well Fare well the sailors
> cruising on Friday nights
> the fruity streets of Soho
> under the gory lights
> gunning for beds or brandies
> or a middle-aged spectacled queer
> the roly poly all night long,
> the breakfast of a beer.
>
> GEORGE BARKER

David Archer had opened his new bookshop at last. It was a splendid place at the Shaftesbury Avenue end of Greek Street. I included Archer in an article in a series for the *Evening Standard* called 'Crisis in the Booktrade' (a foolish title for there has never been a moment when there was *not* a crisis in the booktrade), which was published on 1 May 1956. 'A bookshop should be more than a bookshop,' he declared blissfully. 'It should be a place where folk can come for a cosy chat.' He was in his element, though it was far from easy having a cosy chat. Something was wrong with the door, which was wedged by a wooden block, and the harder I pushed from the outside, the more firmly it stuck, with Archer miming furiously behind the glass, enraged by the malice of inanimate objects. When he loosened the wedge at last, he opened the door indignantly:

'Dear me,' he said as he shot it a hostile glance and ushered me inside, 'I'm *sick* of that door.'

Now he was more like the courteous headwaiter of a grand establishment as he bowed politely to the customers, an invisible napkin draped across his gammy arm, except that he did not like them to part with their money. He loved books so much that it hurt him to sell them. He broke off impatiently when a stranger came up to the desk wanting to pay.

'Are you *sure* you want to buy this?' he asked.

'Yes,' said the man uncomfortably, as if he were buying pornography.

'Ah, well.' Archer accepted the payment under protest, muttering, 'It's our only copy and I'm sure they've lots of the stuff at Better Books.' Rival bookshops, like Better Books and Foyle's, should have paid him a retainer.

After the man hurried out, never to return, Archer continued with his declaration of the bookshop's real objective: 'We have a *duty* . . . we have pictures,' he gave a circular wave, 'and a gallery downstairs where we're holding an exhibition of Deakin's photos, *if* he can be bothered to produce them, and poetry readings, a library where people can browse with daily newspapers and magazines, and a coffee-bar at the back, *not* Espresso.'

'How much has all this cost?' I asked, for the furnishings were certainly first class, but this was not a question which David wanted to hear. 'Hmm, I'm rather edgy about finance.' He hesitated, shifting his feet, 'about £3,000.'

'How does it differ from the old shop?'

'Dear me!' he exclaimed, brightening visibly. 'In 1933 you mean? That was just a hole-in-the-corner thing. This time we're going to specialise in poetry and criticism. And I'm going to publish, too.'

This was the glorious thing about David: he might have seemed a dilettante but he put his flair for spotting talent into practice. The old Parton Press had published work by our finest poets *before* they were widely known: George Barker, *Thirty Preliminary Poems*, 1933; Dylan Thomas, *19 Poems*, (with the Sunday Referee) 1934; David Gascoyne, *Man's Life is This Meat*, 1935; W. S. Graham, *Cage Without Grievance*, 1942.

The new Parton Press confirmed that Archer had not lost his ability to recognise talent, publishing the first work by a young

Indian poet Dom Moraes, which was dedicated to Henrietta who became his wife. *A Beginning* was sufficiently successful to win a literary prize and go into a second edition, though Henrietta dismissed her husband later as 'that twenty-four-hour poet'.

Henrietta worked behind the coffee-bar and prepared the watercress sandwiches:

> All David really wanted was a sort of salon, that's why he wanted a coffee-bar. Strangers used to come off the street, rather attracted by this sort of bookshop, and he'd say, 'Hey, don't ask me about that, I mean there's a very good shop up the road called Foyle's, go there.'
>
> I used to shout and scream at him, 'Don't be so idiotic. Of course we can sell them those books,' but he wasn't interested in commerce.

When Archer told me that he would succeed on a weekly turnover of £140, he admitted that this would leave him nothing for himself. With Deakin helping himself generously to the till when Archer's back was turned, an example others were quick to follow, I began to wonder how the beautiful bookshop could survive.

The bookseller Ben Weinreb had worked for Archer in the old days and they met again when David was considering the second bookshop: 'He'd come into some more money,' Ben Weinreb remembered. 'I think it was the third batch. I never quite knew where it came from; I think this time it was from an aunt. He wanted to start another bookshop and would I help him, would I advise him. Yes, indeed I would. My advice was don't, David, please *don't*. Oh, it was going to be all right *this time*.'

People seldom take advice that they do not want to hear, and David wished to fulfil his fantasy. If someone had accused him of preferring the illusion to the reality, I am sure he would have agreed, and why not? It was nicer. His friend Julian Abercrombie remembered that he really did worry more about the coffee-bar than the books: 'He talked more about the way that people would sit around and there would be wonderful conversation, and the thing that he never talked about was whether it would pay for itself. The point of the bookshop was to be a centre for David, because he wasn't just a person who went round being altruistic. All the people he was kind to gave to David. David lived through other people.'

Julian Abercrombie had known David Archer when he ran the cultural centre in Glasgow during the war. Archer had taken a massive 'working-class flat' with no bathroom but a number of large rooms where poets and painters lived without paying rent. The rooms revolved around a kitchen which had a table and chairs and warmth and they stayed up half the night discussing 'The Waste Land' or listening to Sydney Graham reciting his latest poetry. The catalyst was Archer:

> He didn't talk very much but he liked looking on and listening and enjoying the company of people of all kinds. He had relationships on every level. I think in a way he was always looking for love, but he was also looking for friendship. He liked men and women on different levels and of different ages; he liked young people very much – very excited by young people. Sailors used to come to the Centre and he liked sailors, there was always a sailor or two, coming or going in this tenement; once there were six sitting round the table. He told me once, apropos of the sailors, that he'd never been robbed, never been treated unkindly, never been cheated, and that I can well believe because that's how he behaved to other people.

Julian Abercrombie was delighted that the new bookshop in Greek Street was 'almost the equivalent of the Glasgow Centre', though alarmed to find Archer jumping up and down on the petty-cash box trying to extract some money. As for the sailors, I assume that George Barker had David in mind when he wrote of the 'middle-aged spectacled queer', but this was not an aspect of Archer that I saw for myself, though his intense interest in young people remained. David gained simple pleasure when he was able to bring people together who might have something in common, and on Saturday afternoon on 24 May 1956 he introduced me with a clumsy flourish to a young man with glasses who was wearing a polo-neck sweater: 'He's written a book which is published

tomorrow,' he explained proudly. 'I think the two of you should
. . . *meet*.'

The young man was Colin Wilson, who became a vital part of
my life over the next few months and remains one of my closest
friends. The book was *The Outsider*. By the Monday he was famous,
after it was acclaimed by Toynbee and Connolly, the leading
critics in England at the time.

One morning Archer asked me if I had heard of the 'Bin Book'
he was planning.

'Dust-bins?' I asked him vaguely.

'Of course not,' he snapped impatiently. 'Loony bins. I want to
have them investigated. I'm going to make certain that conditions
are really good by the time I get there.' Ironically he must have
faced reality at last.

The beautiful bookshop closed a few months later. I do not
remember him referring to this, nor did he seem upset. Perhaps he
regarded the failure as inevitable; more likely he had the gallantry
to conceal his disappointment.

Archer worked briefly in another bookshop for Diana Johns. She
said:

> He asked me if I could give him a job, and I was rather nervous about
> this because I was very much in awe of him, knowing he'd published
> Dylan, and I came from Swansea. I thought he was mythical almost,
> and then he said, 'Please employ me, you don't have to pay me a lot of
> money' . . . so he came to work in the bookshop. He was very happy
> because that's where he should always have been, in a bookshop, and
> most of his friends came to see him, like John Davenport, Minton and
> Colquhoun and MacBryde – that was rather troublesome. They'd all
> go off to lunch and then he would ask me to cash a cheque and of course
> it would promptly bounce and the bank would be rather noisy about it,
> so I suggested that perhaps I should pay him every day. He thought
> that was very agreeable, and after a while he left.

He surfaced next in the lampshade department in Selfridges.
When I called to see him there, I realised this was tactless for I had

no intention of buying a lamp and he seemed embarrassed, so I did not do so again. Though he tried, he did not really belong. His old-fashioned courtesy disconcerted the customers, and the staff in the lampshade department failed to respond when he attempted to organise a 'cultural group' where people could 'get together and make a go of it'. Paul Potts remembered 'a rather fussy, suburban woman' ordering Archer about, 'very lower-middle class. And when it came to one o'clock he just bowed to her and said, "Excuse me, madam, it's time for my luncheon now so you'll have to excuse me." He didn't say lunch, he said luncheon.'

I heard of him next after Deakin went to see him in a basement room off the Edgware Road where he spent most of his time in bed, surrounded by piles of old newspapers and empty milk bottles. The electricity had been cut off so he read by the light from dozens of candles. 'The effect was rather good,' said Deakin, 'like Versailles.'

Occasionally he reappeared in Soho, still optimistic, still anxious to bring people together, with a grandiose plan to transform St Ives into 'the Venice of the South'.

'I got glimpses of him,' said Maurice Richardson, 'mostly in Soho pubs. Archer – curious how one always thinks of him by his surname only, as if he were an institution, which indeed he was – seemed if anything to be younger, with his pink face and crisp hair. In spite of being broke he was unfailingly cheerful, always interested in other people and their doings, full of sympathy, funny but non-malicious. Twice he asked me for references. One job was moral tutor at an adult education college, the other was night-watchman at a cap factory.'

With the understandable logic of someone who had given away thousands of pounds, he saw nothing wrong in asking for money in return. 'Tap, tap, tap,' said Deakin cruelly, 'you're as bad as Woody-Woodpecker. Francis is fed up with your begging letters.' Archer laughed nervously and it occurred to me that Deakin resented anyone receiving anything which might have gone to himself. His attitude to Archer was curious, almost as if he had no more time for him now that he was broke. When Merilyn Thorold, one of the Colony's popular and regular members, asked him to help with a fund she was organising for Archer, Deakin told her, 'He can die in the gutter for all I care.'

Possibly, Archer was becoming a nuisance. He managed to exasperate Elizabeth Smart, who threw her cheque-book at him: 'I told him I was very poor, and the ceiling was dripping and I had hundreds of problems, and he kept on saying, just *do* and I said *no*, the bank manager, just a pound, well by the time it gets into your . . . I just got into a temper and threw the cheque-book at him and ran upstairs and screamed in the bathroom. And, you know, he was charming and came back with a bunch of flowers.'

In his richer days, Archer, as was his custom, put a five-pound note into an empty matchbox which he slipped into Dom Moraes' pocket. When Dom discovered the matchbox, he threw it away without realising what it contained. Now he tried to start a trust fund for David Archer, who was not the easiest of beneficiaries and resented it when the money was tied up to prevent his usual pillage. When I met him he was far from grateful.

'I'm sick of it,' he complained, 'I don't mind telling you, I don't have much trust in that trust. Phantom Fund, that's what I call it.'

I suggested that people were trying to protect him.

'Everyone seems determined to prevent me from getting any money,' he replied with a loud, sarcastic laugh, describing a visit to his bank manager that morning.

'I'm very suprised to see you here again,' the manager had said.

'Why?' Archer had asked.

'Because only yesterday you came in for a pound.'

'Well, today I want ten shillings.'

'I'm sorry, Mr Archer, it's out of the question.'

'*Really!*' Archer gave me a sidelong look, as if such behaviour was scarcely credible, and another shattering laugh. 'He tries to be a father figure and he's *years* younger than I am. Says it's for my own good. Anyhow, he gave me seven and six in the end. Dear me!'

Yet Archer, in his day a genuine 'benefactor of the arts', to use that hackneyed phrase, had given away an estimated eighty thousand pounds. Now, when he did get his hands on the Fund with Houdini-like cunning, he gave most of it away again. Probably this gave him the greatest pleasure of all, but it brought him further down, to a Salvation Army hostel in Stepney. Merilyn Thorold was dismayed when she met him – 'desperate and threadbare, though neat as always' – and started another fund in the Colony, but by now people were less keen to contribute to someone they seldom saw. The last time I met him was in the Colony on a rare evening out. I thought that, contrary to reports, he looked good. Paler, older and stiffer, he was still erect, smart, and apparently undefeated. His eyes gleamed with pleasure as he watched me having a heated though short-lived argument with Francis Bacon. I was glad that I did not feel sorry for him as he smiled across the room, but this façade was more of an effort than I realised. A few days later, after a young dancer, John MacDonald, gave him some money, he went out for a good dinner and drinks with some friends, wrote thank-you letters to the people who had been kind to him, and killed himself with an overdose of aspirin. He retained his courtesy to the end.

The inquest recorded that 'Mr David Alderley Archer, aged sixty-four, had come down in the world', and decided that the balance of his mind was disturbed, though this was patently not true. The coroner added that 'He was alone, but he had a few friends,' and this was undeniable, except that his friends were legion.

Merilyn Thorold was appalled when someone accused her of indirectly killing him when the weekly supply of money ran out. She was presented with a casket containing his ashes, and received a final note from Archer in a little envelope enclosing a tiny sum of money – 'like one pound fifty' – to go to the family of a boyfriend who had no address. 'I didn't know what to do with it.' The casket sat in her drawing-room for six months before she was able to take it to Castle Eaton, where she had arranged for him to be buried next to his parents. 'It was almost sad seeing the casket go: one had got extraordinarily attached to it. It was very strange that every time I looked at the casket I thought of David and it made me smile.'

The vicar published a short piece about Archer in the parish magazine, which came to the attention of the governor of the school house which had been endowed by Archer's grandfather. Now the school was closed and the substantial endowment was no longer needed.

'I am so sorry to learn of Mr Archer's death,' wrote the governor to Merilyn. 'We had been trying to contact him for some time to ask if he could make use of the money himself.'

When Maurice Leitch asked me to narrate the BBC Radio 4 tribute to David Archer, he chose *A Gentleman of Soho* for the title. It was the perfect description.

Caitlin Thomas and the Television Interview

That meeting with Colin Wilson in Archer's bookshop changed the course of my life, launching me on a new career as a television interviewer. I had decided to go back to sea, when I happened to meet Peter Hunt in the French pub and he mentioned that he needed interviewers for the weekly ITV programme *This Week* which he produced and asked me if I would like to be one. Assuming that this was idle Saturday night pub talk, I agreed instantly – 'I'll call at your office on Monday morning' – and he shied off in alarm as I expected. However, he renewed his invitation a few days later and I joined Associated Rediffusion in September 1956; Colin Wilson became the first person I interviewed in a short film for *This Week* which I scripted myself. Reviewing it in the *Sketch* the next morning, Herbert Kretzmer wrote: 'Colin (I'm a genius) Wilson gives me a pain.' Oblivious to the possible harm to Colin, I was thrilled.

For the only time in my life I was in the right place at the right moment. My interview with Colin led to another with Cecil Beaton and a third with Paul Getty – 'I wouldn't say millionaires are mean, they simply have a healthy respect for money.' Soon I graduated to 'live' interviews, which were so terrifying that I still feel a frisson of fear when I hear the title music of the Karelia Suite by Sibelius which meant I was 'on'. Afterwards I fled to Soho in order to unwind.

I was lucky. I was not on the staff and interviewers came and went swiftly, but the managing director, a retired admiral, approved of my plummy accent and his wife approved of my haircut. When I interviewed two amateurs who sailed across the Atlantic in a cockleshell and had to be rescued, I praised their courage but accused them of exhibitionism, which produced the heading over Milton Shulman's review in the *Standard*, 'Mr Farson Pulls No Punches', which impressed the producers considerably.

Then Deakin nearly wrecked it all.

Though everyone 'knew' Dylan Thomas 'intimately', I met him only once, at lunchtime in the York Minister where he sat silently, plainly suffering from a terrible hangover. He was flying to New York later that day and the only time he brightened was when he noticed that the magazine I was carrying contained an unpublished novelette by Raymond Chandler, and he asked me if he could take this for the flight.

I found his wife, Caitlin, more formidable, especially when I met her again in the Caves a year or so later when she was understandably distraught, on the point of flying to New York to see Dylan who was dying. Deakin clucked around her, stating that *he* understood what she was going through, with, as was his wont, the implication that this was a privilege reserved for himself, which so enraged her that she seized a bottle and brought it down with all her force on top of his head. His skull would have split like a melon had he not dodged, and a visible dent was left on the wooden counter where her missile shattered into fragments.

Consequently, I was suspicious when Deakin suggested towards the end of 1956 that Caitlin would be a perfect subject for *This Week* in view of the publication of *Dylan Thomas in America* by John Malcolm Brinnin, in which he described her frantic behaviour at Dylan's bedside as he lay in an oxygen tent and how she seized a crucifix to hit one of the nuns who were trying to restrain her. It was a book which upset many of her friends and I was to give her the chance to reply.

I mentioned the idea casually to Peter Hunt and to my dismay he thought it was excellent. That Friday evening, after endless technical rehearsals, Caitlin made a belated entrance at Television House, escorted by Margaret Taylor and John Deakin, who looked demure yet particularly satanic. I took him aside angrily and accused him of encouraging Caitlin to drink in the Caves earlier in the afternoon. He snapped back that he was hardly in a position to stop her if she insisted on drinking, adding: 'Anyhow, she's perfectly all right, so stop worrying.'

While Deakin knocked back the gin in the hospitality room, scandalising the lady who was deputised to look after the guests with his irreverent comments on everyone connected with the programme, we went downstairs to the studio where Caitlin was slumped in a chair, behaving perfectly, though non-committal to the point of silence.

We returned to the hospitality room where Deakin, who had watched us on the monitor, whispered with relish: 'Fasten your safety-belt, kiddo, it's going to be a bumpy night.'

I moved away, afraid that people would realise that he was a closer friend than the professional acquaintance I pretended.

The producer summoned me to an urgent conference: 'Do we dare take the risk?'

For once I was decisive: 'I am happy to do the interview if you decide to go ahead, but that decision is entirely up to you.'

They hesitated, and I realised that they were mainly concerned with Caitlin's refusal to run through the questions beforehand.

'That man with her,' said Peter Hunt, 'he says she's only playing us up, that she'll be fine when she goes on.'

I groaned inwardly when I thought of Deakin's relish for

disaster, but I came up with a solution: 'If I think she's going to be difficult, I'll say "I'm sorry my questions are upsetting you . . ." and you can move on.'

This satisfied everyone. 'We'll alert the network to look out,' said Peter Hunt, repeating my phrase as the warning signal to anticipate trouble – 'I'm sorry my questions are upsetting you.' Why they failed to cancel the item on the spot I cannot imagine.

We were taken back to the studio and I feared the worst when Caitlin decided at the last moment that she wanted to stand up, which upset the lighting so carefully arranged during the rehearsal, but it was too late to change that now. 'Quiet, studio, good luck, everyone . . .' those familiar, fatal words which made me swallow as my throat went dry. 'Four, three, two . . .' a slashing wave of the arm, a burst of Sibelius, and we were lift-off.

I was careful not to mention her arrival in New York, and the allegation that she had smashed a flower-pot on the statue of the Virgin Mary before she was restrained in a straitjacket, but after some gentle preparatory questioning I did say that many people were distressed by the book.

'Oh, that bloody man,' she exclaimed, shaking her blonde ringlets like a wet Welsh sheepdog, 'he was in love with my husband.'

'I'm sorry my questions are upsetting you . . .'

The camera moved accordingly to the Minister of Health or whoever it was who appeared on the screen, but the sound-man was so enthralled that he forgot to switch over as well, so Caitlin's voice was superimposed over the Minister's face, complaining loudly that she wasn't upset at all: 'What do you mean upset? I want to go on.'

By the time we returned to the hospitality room, the phones were ringing. In the general consternation, Caitlin, Margaret Taylor and Deakin were hurried out of Television House and poured into a taxi.

'Thanks,' I glared as I slammed the door and told the driver to take them to the Caves de France in Dean Street. Deakin smiled back: 'I loved every second.'

Fleet Street was around the corner, and the press arrived in pursuit only seconds later.

The next morning every newspaper ran the story on the front page and I realised that my short-lived television career was over. When I walked up the road, people stopped me to ask about the night before and what had really happened. One man thought that I had handled the interview with tact, another that I had been unnecessarily cruel to that 'poor, distressed woman'. That was the general opinion and when I entered the Caves that Saturday afternoon I found myself in the centre of controversy as people took sides. Constantine Fitzgibbon accused me of upsetting Caitlin and poured an entire pint of beer over my head, so I had to go home and change. I did not bother to go out again. Something else was worrying me: Deakin had phoned me in the morning, absurdly businesslike, to inform me that he had sold a photograph which he had taken during the rehearsal when no one was looking to the *Sunday Graphic*.

As this broke all the rules, I protested: 'Oh no, Deakin, you can't. You've ruined me!'

'Don't be ridiculous,' he replied chirpily, 'I've made you famous. Anyhow, I need the money. Ciao, I've got to run.'

'Well, choose the one which shows me at my best.'

Opening the *Sunday Graphic* the next morning I found his photos spread across the centre pages under the headline 'The Camera That Didn't Cut the Widow'. I thought I looked sympathetic. Most of the Sunday papers included interviews with Caitlin and I was relieved that she did not seem to blame me personally. Also, every reporter made a deliberate if casual mention of drink – she would have been better if given more time, 'said Caitlin Thomas with a glass in her hand', or 'They should have given me a drink before I went on.' Her main concern was the fee: 'Now I'm wondering if, as the programme was faded out, they will suspend the payment. It will be interesting to find out.'

Considering the onslaught of publicity Caitlin behaved impeccably throughout and never reproached me for being – albeit advertently – the cause of it.

The story staggered into Monday's papers as well and I arrived at the office to find several letters of abuse: 'The ham-fisted domineering approach of the "Interrogator" is distasteful. We have seen this person in action before and have wondered why his "victims" have not struck him.' I turned to the next: 'I for one will switch off very promptly whenever he appears for fear of what he will do next.'

'Obviously they're a hoax,' I said hoarsely to my secretary.

She looked pale and concerned: 'I don't think so. I'm afraid they're genuine.'

When I received a summons to go to the Controller of Programmes, I went downstairs as if to my execution. Instead, I received the heartiest congratulations and was looked on with new respect. Thanks to Deakin, I had become a 'TV personality.'

Though I continued to appear on *This Week*, I was given series of my own, such as *Out of Step* and *People in Trouble*. We were filming *Farson's Guide to the British* when our next programme had to be cancelled at the last moment, and as we completed a programme each week this was a momentary crisis. Deakin came up with the instant solution: film a programme in the Caves de France, and call it *Bohemia*. At first this seemed impractical – all those people, and all that noise – until I realised that we could do the interviews before the club opened and the long-shots in the afternoon. At such short notice, it was an advantage to film in one location instead of having to hump the antediluvian equipment all over London. It was only when I went to Australia a few years later, where *Bohemia* had just been shown, that I appreciated how odd the programme must have seemed to outsiders, though I took such people for granted. 'Where did you find all those glorious eccentrics?' I was asked, with wide-eyed admiration. 'In Australia we don't have any at all.'

The 'eccentrics' included Gerald Hamilton. Far from being ashamed of his identification with the disreputable Mr Norris in Isherwood's *Mr Norris Changes Trains*, he had written a book called *Mr Norris and I* and seemed indifferent to the terrible stories told about him: that he escaped conscription by fleeing to Ireland dressed as a nun – 'the Mother Superior', he corrected me – and sold forged passports to the Jews before the war, informing the Nazis before they reached the frontier so that he was doubly rewarded.

'Is it true,' I asked, 'that you are the wickedest man in Europe?'

'Oh, that's very kind of you,' he chuckled, 'wittiest, well, really . . .'

'No, not wittiest, *wickedest.*'

'Well!' he replied with outraged innocence. 'I'm just a harmless old man and when my time comes I shall face my Maker with great confidence.' I expect he bribed his way in.

Other 'eccentrics', rounded up by Deakin with exemplary efficiency, included Eileen Bigland, in a new white hat, a now forgotten writer though a remarkable woman in her day, who spoke of the Himalayas, Moscow, and the beauty of childbirth; Paul Potts, the poet; and Elizabeth Smart, who pulled her hair and made strange faces at the camera. The author of *By Grand Central Station I Sat Down and Wept*, Elizabeth was a true Soho character and one of the most delightful.

There was David Archer, who still had his bookshop then and was so fair that he went full circle as he gave an impassioned plea to publishers to visit such places as the Caves where they could meet struggling poets and painters who needed support. Scrupulous as ever, he added: 'Of course if they did come here they'd only be insulted by drunks and bored by bores so you can't really *blame* them if they stay away, can you?' When he finished he bowed to the startled camera crew – it was the first time this had happened to them. The technicians were impressed by this old-world courtesy, but the editor complained bitterly that Archer was exceptionally difficult to cut 'because he changes his mind in mid-sentence'.

And then there was Deakin himself. Everyone expected the *tour de force* he had been promising all day, a performance to out-Coward Coward, while I prayed that he would not be camp. Instead, suddenly overcome by shyness, he came across like a whimper, as Maurice Richardson commented in his *Observer* review: '. . . the really poignant keynote was struck by that nameless youngish man, the one with the worried face, furrowed like a bloodhound's with wrinkles, he who expressed his unwilling addiction to the Bohemian haunt as due to a craving – an almost oral craving, it seemed – for sympathy.' This must have been disingenuous on Richardson's part for he was a Soho type of person himself, a splendid manic-depressive figure as he haunted the district like Mr Hyde on a one-man orgy from suburbia, and must have known Deakin well.

Bacon on Art in Wheeler's

In 1958 I interviewed Francis on television for a programme called *The Art Game*. He had not been filmed before and refused, at first, unless we paid his bill at Wheeler's. I conveyed his terms to my director, the late Rollo Gamble, an immensely sympathetic man with whom I did my best work for television because he made it such a pleasure. Though it was unknown to settle a bill instead of offering a fee, the idea appealed to Rollo until he discovered, to his horror, that 'Mr Bacon's account' had increased to more than £700, virtually the equivalent of £7,000 today. As the entire budget was a few hundred pounds this was out of the question, but Rollo had the bright idea of seeing Wheeler's owner, Bernard Walsh, and asking for his help. They understood each other at once.

'What fun,' cried Walsh. 'I'll wipe out what Francis owes us and charge it to publicity, so long as you film inside Wheeler's.'

This was what we hoped to do anyhow and Walsh's offer was so generous that Francis could only agree.

In those early days of ITV, the cameras ran out of film after four minutes, so there was much interminable reloading. As we drank copious glasses of champagne throughout the afternoon, when the pieces of film were edited together it looked as if we grew increasingly drunk at astonishing speed.

Having agreed to appear, Francis was at his best. I wish the film existed today, but here is an unedited extract from the end of the typescript (27 August 1958):

D.F.: Do you think there's any point in talking about art at all?

F.B.: Well, it's always a fascinating subject. It's a fascinating subject because people reveal themselves talking about art, not about art, but about their attitude to life and, you know – it's an almost impossible thing . . . because I think Pavlova was right when somebody asked her what she meant when she was dancing the Dying Swan and she said – 'Well, if I could tell you, I wouldn't dance it.'

D.F.: If you could tell about art, would you not paint?

F.B.: Certainly not, because it's something that lies long and far below what is called coherence and consciousness, and one hopes the greatest art is a kind of valve in which very many hidden things of human feeling and destiny are trapped . . . something that can't be definitely and directly said.

D.F.: Your art is often referred to as being sensational. Can you explain that?

F.B.: What do you mean by the word 'senational'?

D.F.: That's the word people often use . . . they're shocked by it, they find it evil, horrifying, unpleasant.

F.B.: I think it is that sometimes I have used subject-matter which people think is sensational because one of the things I have wanted to do was to record the human cry, and that in itself is something sensational. And – but if I could really do it, and it's the most difficult thing to do in art and I wouldn't say I have even been able to do it . . . it would of course be sensational.

D.F.: When you say 'human cry' what do you mean?

F.B.: When I say 'human cry' I mean the whole coagulation of pain, despair.

D.F.: But what about the reverse side of life, Francis, happiness and love? Why paint only despair and pain?

F.B.: Well, happiness and love is a wonderful thing to paint also. I always hope I will be able to do that too. After all, it's only the reverse side of the shadow, isn't it?

D.F.: Does it matter to you that a lot of people are not able to understand your paintings?

F.B.: I don't think you can be interested in whether people understand your paintings or not. After all . . . it's only your own nervous system that you can paint at all. And you know, this is perhaps an aside, but there was a very interesting thing that Valéry said about modern art and it's very true, of course. He said that modern artists want the grin without the cat and by that he meant that they want the sensation of life without the boredom of its conveyance. So the thing is, how can I draw one more veil away from life and present what is called the living sensation more nearly on the nervous system and more violently?

D.F.: And you're the Salome of the modern art world? Taking off the veils?

F.B.: I wouldn't say that, I'm sad to say . . . but of course it would be a very nice thing to be.

D.F.: Have another glass of champagne.

F.B.: Thank you very much, Dan.

Ironically, Francis Bacon has suffered constantly from those admirers who find messages in his work which were never intended. There was one delightful appreciation on television, when an earnest art critic interpreted Bacon's paintings as his reaction to man's inhumanity to man, illustrating this claim with predictable clips of Hitler, Buchenwald and Hiroshima, or similiar clichés of the twentieth century. At least this proved the danger of being arty. In fact, Francis is as fascinated by atrocity as a pathologist is by mutilation, seeing the image rather than the message. He is drawn to carcasses of raw beef because of the colour: 'You've only got to go into a butcher's shop – it's nothing to do with mortality, as people often think, it's to do with the great beauty of the colour of the meat.' It was not the anguish in the famous still from the *Battleship Potemkin* of the screaming nurse with her spectacles shattered which appealed, 'It was the beauty of that shot, the mouth, and I was excited by the idea of it being done in colour, the colour of the lips and the flesh and the tongue.' Surprisingly, this is not a subject he has painted himself, and when he was shown a picture of the still with the nurse's mouth wide open, painted for him especially by Peter Bradshaw, he exclaimed generously, 'The mouth! . . . that's what I've always tried to do.'

In 1956, Francis joined his closest friend Peter Lacey, a former fighter-pilot with a slight, endearing stammer, in Tangier where he had gone to run a bar, but after Francis joined the Marlborough in 1958, he became increasingly preoccupied as the gallery prepared his first retrospective exhibition at the Tate, postponing his return to Tangier where Lacey was ill.

Francis took me to the Tate on the evening before the private view in May 1962, and as we wandered round the empty galleries, I realised that something extraordinary had happened. The following day I flew to Paris to interview James Baldwin for *This Week*, which was now produced by Jeremy Isaacs, and the morning after that I read the English newspapers over my coffee at the Flore and saw that Francis was confirmed as our major British artist. Consequently, it was no surprise when I was confronted by a scene out of Bedlam when I opened the door of the Colony Room that afternoon. For once I was stone-cold sober and it seemed that everyone else was very, very drunk, to an extent that seemed even more maudlin than usual.

'Have you heard the news?' Eleanor Moynihan asked me tearfully.

'Yes, of course,' I replied, 'Francis must be overjoyed.' To my astonishment she slapped me across the face and at this moment Francis freed himself from the crowd surrounding him and steered me towards the lavatory at the back where he told me that among the last of the telegrams he had been receiving all morning was a cable informing him that Peter Lacey had died in Tangier the night before.

A Drink for Mr Deakin

'The worst day in Dan Farson's life was when he met John Deakin.' I learnt of this remark recently. The woman who had made it was an elderly magazine editor whom I respected and she knew Deakin well, though she did not reveal her feelings to me at the time. Though I did not say it, nor do I believe it, she was right in her way, if any such judgement can be correct when it comes from the outside. But in spite of the hangover after the binge, it was worth knowing John Deakin because he made me laugh more than anyone I have met. His laughter was usually destructive, invariably at someone else's expense, but it took the form of irreverence rather than malice. His destructiveness seems more understandable now. Unless I have interpreted it wrongly, he had a terror of insecurity, even of ending up like one of the clochards in his exhibition at David Archer's bookshop in 1956 – 'John Deakin's Paris' – which prompted Colin MacInnes to pay him tribute in *The Times*:

> . . . there are deeper reasons for the compelling power of these images. One is that Mr Deakin has a highly dramatic sense, that borders often . . . on the bizarre, almost the macabre. . . . The other explanation of these photographs lies in the fund of affection and, at times, of pity, that the artist clearly feels for his fellow mortals. Many of those who, all unwittingly, were his sitters, are creatures crushed by life; and the artist, quite without condescension or sentimentality, sees the poignancy of their desperate will to live in a world that has quite defeated them.

Deakin was damned if he was going to be defeated, but he recognised the risk. Façade was all important: the filthy sheepskin overcoat which he wore as if it were mink; the lunches at Wheeler's with Francis, with his caustic remarks about the rich and famous as the members of the Thursday club came downstairs; the Saturday lunchtime 'soirées' at 'Deakin Towers' in Berwick Street where guests arrived as if for an investiture, though armed with bottles – the court jester of Soho would not have appreciated any jest which exposed his vulnerability.

I am sure that Deakin was fond of me, almost obsessively so, but he relished my disasters more than my minor triumphs, which made him almost physically ill, and he needed to cultivate the disasters for his own sense of well-being. Conversely, I was obsessed by his company, taking him to places where I knew that his behaviour would shatter the well-heeled fabric, literally so when he sent the glasses flying.

'It's only gin,' he'd protest indignantly, as Robert Helpmann went down on his hands and knees to mop the priceless Wilton, 'and gin doesn't stain.'

'Don't ever bring that horrible little man here again,' Helpmann whispered severely when we were shown out of the garden basement. Our presence must have been dreaded.

While I worked for *Picture Post*, and he for *Vogue*, we coincided at Brighton on respective assignments to photograph Noël Coward in *The Apple Cart*. I had been there for a couple of days already and Coward could not have treated me more kindly, but Deakin managed to cross him instantly by insisting that they had a mutual friend in common, some junior government official in Nigeria. The more Coward denied this, which he did emphatically, the more Deakin persisted, plainly tipsy from the Brighton Belle.

As the curtain was about to rise, I heard Coward shout at the harassed publicist: 'Never, never let that man near me when I am about to go on stage.'

'Oh dear,' said the publicist when he joined us at the stage door, 'I don't know what you've done but you've upset the Master terribly.'

'Tough shit,' said Deakin with a swing of his Rolleiflex.

'Anyhow,' the man persisted rashly, 'we can give you a box if you'd like to see the play, but you'll have to hurry.'

'Are you mad?' said Deakin. 'I'm taking Mr Farson to see *Soldiers in Skirts* round the corner, he's never seen them before.'

'Oh dear,' said the publicist enviously. 'I wish I could go with you.'

When I left Beauchamp Place for the basement of my grand-mother's house in Pelham Place, Deakin found it less sympathetic for morning coffee because the kitchen was upstairs and the front 'sitting-room' was dark and depressing and unsympathetic. Yet he called unexpectedly from time to time and did so one evening when he was so drunk that he passed out on the sofa which served as a spare bed in the front room. Slightly annoyed by this interruption, as I had been working, I amused myself by drawing a moustache on his face in Indian ink, rather in the French style with twirls at the end, and exaggerated the eyebrows with an upward twist as well. Then I went to my bedroom chuckling at the thought of his surprise when he saw himself in the mirror the next morning. There was one thing wrong with this puerile joke – there was no mirror in the front room.

The next morning he knocked cheerfully on my door, announc-ing, 'I've been to South Ken for a cuppa and the paper. You should have seen the looks people gave me. I must have my sex-boots on today.'

I stared at him, appalled, for the Indian ink had run down his Mickey Mouse face. 'No, Deakin,' I said. 'Look in the mirror.'

He went to the wash-basin and did so. 'Good God!' he exclaimed. 'No wonder they looked at me strangely.'

Disastrous at dinner he was delightful at breakfast, when he talked with a sharpness that was blunted later in the day. For though he posed as a clown with a camera, he was instinctively intelligent. His taste was infallible and if Arthur Jeffress had followed Deakin's advice, his art collection (now in Southampton) would have been outstanding. Where Jeffress bought Paul Delvaux, Deakin would have bought Soutine.

Deakin was a born actor and though many people found him pathetic, he was no more pathetic than Goebbels. He manipulated people with exquisite skill. When a titled young man was foolish enough to introduce Deakin to his new wife, Deakin kissed her hand and rolled his eyes and won her over instantly with an excess of flattery. He knew some secret which the man was terrified he might disclose, probably a former love affair or one that was still continuing, and played on this with the teasing expertise of a fisherman after the fish has bitten. Deakin was far too clever to mention the secret outright, but his lightly veiled asides were only too recognisable to the man who was unable to bear the torture any longer and burst out impetuously, 'Damn you, Deakin, you belong in hell.'

Deakin regarded him with wide-eyed innocence: 'What *can* I have said?'

'Apologise to poor Deakin,' the new wife demanded, and the husband had to do so trying to conceal his rage.

Invariably, Deakin had the last laugh. Once a woman turned on him in the Caves.

'You're evil,' she said.

'I know.'

'You've no thought for anyone except yourself.'

'That's perfectly true.'

'You're mean.'

'Totally.'

'You're . . . well, you're cruel.'

'To a fault.'

As she recited these accusations with increasing desperation, people stopped to listen to Deakin's deadpan agreement, which provoked her further. Finally everyone was laughing so uncontrollably that the poor women fled into the street, hurling the last indictments as she went.

'*Uno* gin, *per favore*,' said Deakin to Carnera, with a gracious bow to the rest of us as he received a round of applause.

Like Archer, I was a willing victim and provided perfect raw material. He would enter the French announcing that he had some sensational piece of news to tell me but would refuse to do so until I bought him a drink. He would arrange to meet me with no intention of turning up. If I liked someone, he would win them over and find their Achilles heel, exposing it so humorously that the friendship could never be the same again. He was the first to support me when he should have attacked, laughing away my laziness and lack of resolve. Every problem could be solved by the simple expedient of another drink. Conversely, I began to resent his successes with a jealousy which was insane, considering how few these were. Indeed, and that was one of the oddest things about him in view of his dread of insecurity, he seemed to have a death-wish as far as his work was concerned after he was sacked from *Vogue*.

This came about when a smart friend gave a party. Deakin had already created rumbles of dissatisfaction after cancelled appointments and two angry scenes with a model, but it was the party that proved his downfall. Deakin arrived at six to assist with the decorations.

'Help yourself to a drink,' waved the friend.

'Do you think I *should*?' Deakin asked with his hand on the bottle. 'Anyhow, what time does it begin?'

'After the show. They should be here by midnight.'

By the time the guests arrived, Deakin was hardly able to see them. 'I dimly remember the moment when I knew I was about to pass out. I handed my glass to someone, Dame Margot or Edith – and slid to the floor. Apparently I had to be carried out like Hamlet at the end of the play.'

When Deakin went up in the *Vogue* lift the next morning, Cecil Beaton stared fixedly in front and refused to speak.

'He was at the party, of course. Everyone knows. It's so shameful.'

'Nonsense, Deakin,' I assured him, giving him typically Deakin comfort. 'Who are they talking about this morning? Helpmann, Beaton, Dame Margot, Dame Edith? No, your name is on everybody's lips.'

'Hmm,' said Deakin, tapping the counter of the bar, 'you may have a point.'

But they gave him the sack and from then on he referred to himself as 'the ex-*Vogue* photographer', though he did so in such a grandiose manner that it gave him an extra chic. His photography was never the same again and there were times when he seemed to sabotage his own best interests. Occasional portrait commissions proved so unflattering that we ached with laughter when we saw the prints. The results were rejected so often by the sitters that Deakin learnt to ask for his fee in advance – 'for expenses, you understand' – but it was hardly lucrative. There was a moment when it seemed that security had caught up with him, in spite of his efforts to elude it, when he landed a highly paid job in advertising. A friend in the agency took the risk of recommending Deakin for a massive new campaign for Players cigarettes, yet Deakin did not have his heart in it, responding to this threat of prosperity as a prisoner dreads the outside world on his release. Considering his basic fear of insecurity, this did not make sense when he was being offered a fee of several hundred pounds, the equivalent of thousands today. Maybe he thought that such photographs were beneath him; certainly he took remarkably little trouble, substituting Hyde Park for the English countryside location he had been asked for. He used a young friend and Virginia Law as his models and the photographs proved splendid in the hurried circumstances, except for one glaring error: the man was holding a packet of Senior Service.

Armed with the requisite packets of Players, Deakin took the photographs again, this time in the setting of a Chinese garden or 'floral fairyland' as he called it, but when I saw him in the French pub on the appointed day all he had bought as props was a lantern from the Chinese food store in Wardour Street and a potted plant from Berwick Market. And he seemed to be covered in snowflakes.

'I've been whitewashing my patio,' he explained, referring to the narrow area of his basement.

'I thought they wanted a Chinese garden?'

'By the time I'm through they won't know the difference. God, is that the time?' but he ordered another Pernod and by the time he returned to his 'patio' he found a disgruntled group of elegant copywriters and clients waiting for him, pressed *away* from the wet whitewashed walls which had ruined a couple of coats already.

Falling down the area steps, he collided with the lonely hired arc-light, already tall and precarious, which crashed across the 'patio', shattering the glass, narrowly missing the male model who ran up the steps screaming that he would never work with 'that photographer' again.

'They fired me with alacrity,' said Deakin glumly as he recounted the episode later. Then he found the perfect niche.

'Do you know this photographer, Deakin?' Anthony Armstrong-Jones asked me.

'Very well indeed.'

'He must lead an extraordinary life.'

'Extraordinary?' I replied cautiously. 'What exactly do you mean?'

'All those trips to Hollywood . . .'

'To *where*?' I interrupted incredulously.

'Didn't you see his photographs of Sinatra in last week's *Sunday Times*? And who was it the week before . . . ?' I started to laugh, explaining that Deakin attended the press shows, sitting in the front row, to the irritation of Dilys Powell who was short-sighed, and clicked away at the screen. Then he presented the picture editor with an exclusive 'still' which was published with her review.

'You don't mean it!' said Armstrong-Jones with admiration. 'I didn't realise it was technically possible.'

Increasingly restless in London, Deakin persuaded me to let him visit my parents' home when I was staying with them in North Devon. Since I knew how disastrous a guest he could be, it was sheer folly to introduce him to one's mother and father and proof of my crass naïvety. A letter from London, asking if he could escape for just a few days, was so pathetic that I said we would meet the train. We met several trains, only to return home to find a belated message that Deakin had missed them the other end. When he arrived at last, he fell out, picked himself up and greeted my mother: 'My God, Mrs Farson, I'd never have come if I'd known it was going to take so long.' I could tell from her expression that I had made a bad mistake.

Deakin looked awful in the clear Devon light. There was tea on the lawn when we arrived at the Grey House with two neighbours who had dropped in unexpectedly, and Deakin's eyes were so bloodshot in the sunlight that the guests averted their own when they were introduced. His tongue was an even nastier shade of aubergine than usual. My father recognised another alcoholic on sight, and stiffened.

Far from being witty as I had hoped, Deakin's conversation was camp and outré, mystifying the neighbours who left quickly. He followed me into the kitchen, announcing, 'I'm dying for a drink.'

My mother was refilling the teapot and explained that there was no drink in the house apart from a bottle of sherry disguised as vinegar which had resulted in a revolting trifle a few days earlier when the bottles were confused.

'Sherry would be delicious, Mrs Farson,' said Deakin primly, and it was poured into a delicate white-and-gold Rockingham teacup with a slice of lemon floating on the top to make it more convincing.

'Mr Deakin wanted lemon tea,' my mother explained when we returned, but my father scented the truth with a single sniff and phoned for a taxi.

While my father set out on a three-day 'bender', Deakin decided that he was there for the good of his health and refused another drop, even when my father reeled back from the pubs armed with bottles. The following day, Deakin sat outside in a deckchair like an invalid on board ship, his face tilted to the sun, while my father coughed and groaned and disappeared as soon as he had the strength to phone for another taxi.

After Deakin departed my father recovered and declared vehemently: 'I never want to see that man near this house again.'

'Hear, hear!' endorsed my mother, echoing the sentiments of so many before her. Surprisingly, my father met him again on a rare visit to the French during one of his own disastrous visits to London. Deakin had his camera – 'I thought that's an interesting face' – but failed to recognise my father until he had taken his photograph. At that moment my father looked up and was so relieved to find someone he knew that they drank together for the rest of the evening in Soho. The news dumbfounded both my mother and myself.

'That Deakin!' exclaimed my father, lying in bed at Pelham Place. 'You've got to hand it to him. He's got something. Goddammit – I quite *like* the man.'

Seeking escape, Deakin went to Italy. Of all the places he had been to, I believe that Deakin was fondest of Rome, where the Italians relished his sense of mischief, apparently treating him like an attendant clown or mascot. Somehow he raised the fare to go there and wrote happily from a rented flat with a balcony decorated with plants in whitewashed tins. Deakin was still in Italy when I flew to Australia, where I spent several months filming *Farson in Australia*. My father had died and I wrote to my mother suggesting that she join me for a holiday in the Mediterranean on my journey back. The idea did not appeal to her, so, with a feeling of guilty relief, I managed to contact Deakin and stopped off in Rome instead. Starved of frivolity in Australia, the only quality lacking, I was thankful to see him again, while Deakin said it was like a release from prison. I was not too sure what had gone wrong, but the first Roman Spring had ended unhappily and Deakin had sought refuge with an old friend called Gianni, a fashion designer who lived in the north of Italy, who welcomed him into his family, even paying a modest sum for his help with Gianni's forthcoming collection. Deakin was far from grateful.

'He's worse than Hitler,' he complained bitterly. 'Never lets me out of his sight. You've no idea how hard it was to escape. As for that hideous wife, and that dreadful Alsatian dog which is in love with me . . .'

'Oh, Deakin!' I laughed. It was good to see him again.

For the next three days everything was perfect: the hotel he had chosen for me; the friends he introduced me to; the open-air restaurants where we talked the afternoon away; his favourite places, like the catacomb with thousands of skulls; even an empty nightclub where the orchestra played luscious, sentimental Neapolitan songs. I had money saved from my salary while I filmed in Australia, and though Deakin and I drank continually we did so without the threat of curfew. They were days of pure relaxation and laughter.

At one point he drummed the table and remarked, too casually, 'By the by, you *do* know that I am married?'

'Married!' The bombshell had the desired effect.

'As a matter of fact I have two step-sons in Australia.'

'You're not serious?'

'Why not? You surprise me, child. Don't you realise, I am irresistible . . .'

'No, seriously. Please . . .'

'Buy me a drink and I'll tell you.'

While he was still in Rome, a man approached him in his favourite bar and asked if he was married.

'Is this a proposal?' said Deakin archly, but the Italian did not understand.

'You are single, right?'

Deakin nodded.

'Well, I have this lady who wants to marry you.'

'Marry me? Is she a crazy person?'

'On condition the man does not ask his marital rights. She do not wish to sleep with you or ever see you again.'

'Really,' said Deakin with a lift of his eyebrows as he lowered his glass. 'You interest me strangely, child. Pray tell me more.'

The woman was not Italian; she had been Hungarian but now she was 'stateless'. There were many such women who needed passports but she was in a happier position than most, having brought her jewels when she escaped after the uprising. Now she was tired and scared of the knock on the door at midnight and the constant threat of arrest on some minor technicality, which is why she was offering five hundred dollars to any man who would marry her, preferably an Englishman.

'All expenses paid?' asked Deakin, for the lady lived in Milan.

'Yes, my friend is a generous woman.'

On the evening that Deakin waited for her in the foyer of a grand hotel, he had his doubts. 'It seemed so ignominious, at my age. I expected a hideous old bag dressed in black bombazine and thought I must be mad until I heard this voice behind me – "Mr John Deakin?" – and turned round to see this really elegant woman.'

'This is for you,' Anna had said in the taxi, handing him an envelope as they drove to a pre-nuptial dinner. 'I always think it nicer when the husband pays.'

'You're so understanding,' Deakin replied with growing admiration.

The future Mrs Deakin had reserved a table at the best restaurant in Milan and told him over their meal of her vulnerability.

'Only the other night the police burst into my apartment demanding to see my papers. It is so shaming. With a passport, I shall be secure.'

Deakin asked if she had been married before.

'Twice. You have two step-sons in Australia and a daughter in Brazil. And you?'

'Never. This is my first.'

'I thought you would be different . . .'

'Really,' he smiled, 'how?'

'Oh, I don't know, perhaps,' she had blushed slightly, 'more "on the make", a gigolo as they say.'

Deakin looked suitably hurt and she rested her hand on his reassuringly. 'Now I can see you are not like that at all.'

The next day had started uncomfortably with a visit to the British consular representative, who happened to have known Deakin before and greeted him effusively.

'Well, I must say, this is good news!' Arranging the various forms in front of him, he asked: 'And how long have you known the good lady?'

'Since yesterday,' said Deakin.

When the official learnt that the 'good lady' was stateless and fifty-seven, his enthusiasm had faded. 'I see, I never thought you were the marrying kind.'

Deakin had been thankful when the civic ceremony was over and he was able to relax with a glass of wine at his wedding breakfast afterwards.

'All the Hungarian colony were there. It was rather touching how they rejoiced in her good fortune as she showed them the brand-new passport and they handed it around as if it was the rarest diamond in the world. The wine and food flowed. They were all terribly nice to me, thanking me so much. I was quite embarrassed, especially when her lawyer took me aside – I suspect they were having an affair – and gave me the envelope with the five hundred dollars. Do you know, I'd been thinking of nothing else but those five hundred smackers and how they'd replace the Rollei that some bastard pick-up had stolen, and now I felt I couldn't go through with it. I handed the envelope back.'

'You didn't!'

'Of course I didn't. But the thought did occur to me. You see, she was so kind to me.'

Deakin shook his head from side to side, grimacing as if a bee had flown into his ear. 'When she heard I was catching the train back to Rome, she insisted I fly in order to arrive in time for "the cocktails". They saw me off at the airport and when I said goodbye to her, she whispered, "I think, Mr Deakin, you are the nicest husband I have ever had." '

So Deakin returned to Rome in style in his crumpled pale-blue suit with the pink Chianti stains and his small TWA bag with his spare shirt and razor and the precious envelope with the money for a new camera. Arriving in time for 'the cocktails' as intended, he joined a group of friends and explained his absence. When he finished, Peter Ustinov said that there was one thing left to do: insert a notice in the 'Births' column of *The Times*: 'To John and Anna Deakin, a Rolleiflex was born.'

Either the camera was not replaced, or it was stolen again, for he

had to borrow a camera on the rare occasions when he needed one
after his return to London. Photography no longer interested him,
so he turned to painting instead. It was typical of Deakin, who was
one of the most sophisticated people alive, that he should pass
himself off as a 'naïf' and be sold, as such by the Portal Gallery
which specialised in the genuine article. While his enthusiasm
lasted, he worked on his 'sophisticates' with meticulous care,
hanging Queen Mary with pearls, tattooing sailors, embellishing
still-lifes with imaginary flowers. The results were highly decorative and bought for increasing sums. On a visit to the Victoria and
Albert Museum in 1985, I went to the bookstall to buy some
postcards and my eye was caught by a picture that could only have
been his, that of a pearly queen adorned with hundreds of precise
sequins and a hat with abundant pink feathers. Sure enough this
was revealed as 'John Deakin. *Pearly Queen*. Collection Van
Bloemen. Portal Gallery. London'. As if he feared commercial
success, Deakin abandoned his 'naïfs' at the moment when they
might have earned him a living, and turned to collages instead.
Whereas an exhibition of the 'naïfs' could have been appealing, the
collages gave the definite and correct impression that they had
been turned out slickly without much effort, though I retain a
fondness for a small collage of an eye superimposed on a poached
egg on toast; and the fact that the newsprint is now showing
through the yolk adds an interesting dimension. However, most of
the collages were large assemblies of fruit and veg with insects
crawling about and eyes looming ominously, with trendy titles like
Mr Lionel Bart and *Miss Joan Littlewood*.

'When they see their names at the Vernissage, they won't be
able to resist them.' But resist them they did, with prices ranging
from £100 to £250, though I bought a collage of myself with my face
on the cover of an Australian *TV Times*, topped by a gigantic
cauliflower like a head-dress.

There was one review: 'I only hope,' wrote the art critic in the
Daily Mail, 'that the painter's optimism will not be matched by the
public's enthusiasm.' Nor was it. So Deakin turned to dolls' heads

instead, returning from the Dolls' Hospital laden with fractured heads which he painted and covered with the transfers of ferns, superimposed on the heads like veins. Lunching with Francis at Wheeler's he spat out a vertebrae from a mouthful of steamed turbot and eyed it with approval: 'I say, this would look rather good on one of my dolls' heads.' From then on, fish bones or oxtail bones were part of the motif, especially if one side of the doll's face was missing, when they would be stuck inside.

When he tired of the dolls' heads, which he did fairly quickly, he turned to his monsters. These were huge, ungainly Yeti-like figures made from buckets of papier-mâché and chicken wire, gradually filling the small room in 'Berwick Strasse' where Deakin brought friends to inspect them, including a drunken Irishman who promptly collapsed on Deakin's bed, waking later to find himself surrounded in the twilight by the monsters *and* Deakin – 'He fled down the stairs without so much as a thank you!'

On his last visit to the Grey House in Devon after my parents' death, Deakin talked of the monsters with affection.

'How nice they would look,' he suggested, 'dotted about in your little wood. You could see them peering through the branches.'

Dubiously, I pointed out that their transport would be too expensive. Where are the monsters now? I think of them from time to time, wondering about the sensation they must have caused when Deakin's irate landlord threw them into Berwick Street to unnerve the late-night stragglers of Soho or bewilder the refuse men at dawn.

Because so much of his own work has vanished, it is a consolation that Lucian Freud painted his portrait, collecting him at dawn day after day, keeping him quiet with relays of retsina while he sat for him. One lunchtime Deakin staggered into the French ashen-faced and told me that Lucian was unhappy with the portrait and had torn it up. 'Now we've got to start all over again and I don't know if I can stand it.' I owned the final portait to begin with, a fine example of Lucian Freud's ability to see beneath the surface. Exhibited with other portraits at the time, it was reproduced in the *Daily Telegraph* under the heading, 'Studies of Compelling Nastiness', a cutting which Deakin brandished with personal pride.

It was hardly surprising if he yearned to escape but when he tried to sober up in Soho it was hideous to behold. Deakin was the only person I knew in Soho who was wildly entertaining when drunk and insufferable when he decided to be sober. On these rare occasions, his system shuddering from the shock and his outraged nerves screaming to be calmed with the first drink of the day, he continued to haunt the pubs. Severe as a schoolmistress suffering from a cold, he sat sedately with a tomato juice or read a paper without buying anything at all. From time to time he would glance at the depraved behaviour of yesterday's friends and shake his head with a sad expression, implying, 'Father forgive them, they know not what they do.' If one dared to offer him a drink, he looked as offended as the cook who is asked to wash the front steps when the daily falls ill. Politely, he'd decline as if such a thought was beneath his dignity. His friends started to avoid him, but at this point he would pursue them with inane chatter – 'Oh it's so wonderful to feel so well. I can't imagine how you can drink day after day like that. I got up early this morning and set to work cleaning "Deakin Towers". I scrubbed the floors and swept the carpets. Then I did all my washing, boiled my socks and four shirts. Everything's as clean as a new pin. I've just bought some liver, so cheap compared to' – he'd glare accusingly at the other person's glass – 'a whisky which is two-and-six. Now I'm off to a film and then an early night for me.' And he'd exit triumphantly.

Persuaded to have lunch at Wheeler's, he might toy with some caviar when tempted to by Francis on the grounds that 'It's so health-giving', yet flinch with horror from a glass of champagne. Then he would leave suddenly: 'No, I'm afraid I'm not in a speaking mood, that's all. No, I just prefer my own company,' and would sweep out looking livid in his old sheepskin coat. On such occasions, his presence at the banquet was as disturbing as Banquo's. When he returned to his old self, as he did invariably after two days, the whole of Soho sighed with relief; there is no one Soho dislikes more than a reformed drunk, but this meant that Deakin was forced back into the role of jester.

Possibly because he resented my life-line to Devon, he was brutal when my life fell apart. I had done too much, too soon. I moved into Limehouse before it was fashionable; ran a pub on the Isle of Dogs where I lost most of my money; and became that most specious of creatures – a 'TV celebrity'. I was photographed and caricatured, and after one programme, *Living for Kicks*, which made front-page news as the Brighton police investigated the 'Sexpresso' bar where a teenager dared to say that he believed in sex before marriage, a magazine reported: 'It took one programme to do what months of steady interviewing failed to do – make him, Dan Farson, a BIG TV personality . . . suddenly made him an international celebrity. Learned Sunday papers now print profiles of him. Currently the talk around TV studios is: After this Dan can demand the biggest salary any TV star ever had.'

It was time to move on. My parents had left me the house in North Devon and I thought it was madness to go there for only a few weeks in the year. Above all, I wanted to find out if I could write. At first Associated Rediffusion refused to accept my resignation but when they realised that I was serious they allowed me to break my contract, but I left under a cloud, for people could not believe that I had thrown up such a job of my own accord.

Professionally I had committed suicide. Within a horrifyingly short space of time, my money ran out, though I made the occasional visit to London as a freelance.

As I drank in the Kismet Club one afternoon with Deakin after I had been charged with being drunk and disorderly in Limehouse that morning, I was thankful not to see my name in the evening papers as it would have been before. But it made the last edition. For some reason, the magistrate had offered me 'time to pay', hardly necessary for a fine of a few shillings, and the item was headed: 'Dan Farson Asks for Time to Pay'. Deakin read this with unconcealed satisfaction and when I returned to Devon a friend wrote that he was celebrating in Soho because the 'ex-telly star had to ask for time to pay: how have the mighty fallen!'

I had the solace of the sea and my life in Devon where I returned to a semblance of sanity. I missed the rest of the Swinging Sixties and towards the end of that overrated decade I happened to meet Deakin in the Golden Lion soon after opening time. He was sober and almost contrite.

'I didn't do much to help, did I?'

'No.' It seemed pointless to say otherwise.

What I did mind was his calculated attempt to undermine my friendship with Francis Bacon, which was easy to achieve in my absence. 'Out of sight, out of mind' is one of the truer clichés. Miss Beston, who looks after Bacon's work at the Marlborough, seemed surprised when I met her years later: 'You're not what John led me to expect at all.' Deakin went to considerable lengths to hammer such a wedge. Possibly he failed to appreciate how rewarding the balance between the three of us had been.

I received reports of his visits to hospital without much alarm, for I knew how he relished hospitals, treating them like hotels where he could hold court. A friend described a visit to the homoeopathic ward at Homerton where Deakin was being treated for some suspected tropical disease: 'A hell of a journey. The first thing I did was pour myself a glass of water and I nearly choked. His decanter was full of neat gin. God knows how he does it, but he seems to be having a ball.' The hospital could not discover what was wrong with him, so he discharged himself in order to go to Paris for the opening of the Francis Bacon exhibition at the Grand Palais (1971), an occasion I ached to go to myself but I had not been invited and could not afford it. I gathered that nerves were being stretched as the day approached.

The model for most of the paintings was George Dyer, a charming, hopeless man who was close to being an alcoholic, one of those lovable people who seem beyond redemption – which is one reason, paradoxically, why they are lovable. Once, George arrived at the Grey House in Devon at eight o'clock in the morning in a car filled with friends who had driven from a Soho club called the Apollo. George, who frequently looked half asleep, stumbled out and blinked with surprise as he saw the empty sands below – 'I thought we were going to Brighton,' he explained.

His manners were impeccable. He was far more of a gentleman in his way than the minor villain that he was claimed to be, though I am certain that he could be desperately bad news to those who were closest to him. Once he threatened to throw himself out of the window of a New York hotel, but withdrew when he was told to jump: 'It's the twenty-fifth storey so you won't feel a thing.' Another time he caused considerable trouble when he phoned the police anonymously with information which led to a raid for drugs in the mews house where Francis lived.

Now Deakin wrote to me that he had quarrelled with Francis after a 'strained lunch at Wheeler's where George was morose and not drinking in readiness for Paris'.

On the evening of the grand opening with a military guard lining the courtyard below, Francis Bacon waited at the top of the staircase to welcome President Pompidou when word was brought that George Dyer had been found on the lavatory in his hotel bedroom with blood pouring from his nose and mouth having committed suicide. With this knowledge, Francis had to receive the President after a fanfare of trumpets and, with a brutal irony, one of the first paintings they stopped at was a triptych of *Three Figures in a Room* with one of the panels showing George Dyer on the lavatory.

If the fates had taken their retribution with Lacey's death on the opening of the Tate exhibition, they exacted a terrible vengeance now, which helps to explain Bacon's indifference to the trappings of success and his contemptuous rejection of the honours offered him.

Bacon's astonishing *Triptych May–June 1973* narrates George Dyer's suicide; a moving record of his friend and model.

Deakin's reaction to the tragedy was extraordinary. Inevitably, he had forgotten the quarrel and wrote that he was 'received in triumph at the top of the grandest of all grand staircases', though after the celebrations he had been forced to return to the Homerton Hospital again. By this time he was in an appalling condition, which goes some way to explain the letter he wrote at that time:

The Paris histoire could not have been less like your imaginings. Far from nightly dancing the Merry Widow waltz at Maxim's until dawn, ospreys in my hair and my throat ablaze with diamonds, it is a tear-jerker of unparalleled misery. To begin with my illness had reached its climax (necessary details to give you the true picture) mouth and throat full of ulcers, unable to eat, poisoned big toe oozing pus, itching blisters around my arse, and my prick skinned and raw. I had been having treatment for eight weeks and was due to be hospitalised but put it off until after the opening. After two weeks here, now everything under perfect control and much to Francis's annoyance had nothing to do with drink or, as the doc put it so delicately, my social life.

After describing his personal triumph in Paris – 'four days were spent in a blur of brandy, illness and purple hearts' – he ended optimistically:

I am here for another two weeks I think. But you know me. I use it like others use Aix les Bains or Elizabeth Arden's Health Farm. Yours, John.
    P.S. If you happen to have a 'My life with Lana Turner' (or somesuch) written by a secretary-companion wrongfully dismissed with a week's notice after having devoted twenty selfless years to her. If not – sit down and write one for me. The condition of the sale of the movie rights being that I play the embittered spinster companion – naturally!
    P.P.S. How's about George's demise!

I could hardly credit this. He was one of George's champions, and was that all the tragedy meant to him? Perhaps this brittle response concealed a greater anxiety about himself. Though I have a massive mistrust of experts, I was stunned to learn that they had been giving him the wrong treatment. Deakin had lung cancer, though this seemed alien to the symptoms he described. (I have learnt since that he had a skin infection and cancer too.) With gallant flippancy, helped by his relish for hospital life, he wrote to me from the Westminster Hospital, in the Marie Celeste Ward, a name which he appreciated in all its irony, describing the visitors with their

> signed copies, champagnes, the vintage port, the Fine Champagne cognac, flowers everywhere. The whole thing was out of hand and exhausting. I adored your telegram particularly after the public statement in the Colony: 'I hope to God he dies under the knife tomorrow.' History does not relate what the people who do not know either of us thought. Stiches out today so not too bad.
>
> P.S. A kiss for Little [my dog Littlewood, a marvellous mongrel of whom he was fond].

This was written on 11 April 1972 after his operation, which was termed 'successful': 'An *early* cancer, all removed'. Already he was enthusiastic over plans to live in the Greek island of Poros in a balconied place on the harbour arranged for him by an American friend known as Black Patch because of the eye-patch he wore, and paid for by Francis Bacon. With my own financial situation improving, I set out for Romania to research a book on my great-uncle, Bram Stoker, duly published as *The Man Who Wrote Dracula*, and when this journey ended I flew to Athens and caught the ferry from Piraeus to Poros. Deakin had urged me to join him and settle permanently on Poros myself: 'Now there's no need to purse your lips in bitter envy. Because all you have to do is poison all the dogs, sell Tobacco Road and live happy ever after on the proceeds. If this goes against the grain, then bring the dogs – so simple.'

As the steamer approached the harbour, I scanned it for that familiar figure but there was no sign of him. After a swim, I returned in the evening, hoping to be guided by the sound of his laughter. The next morning I visited the police station but they knew of no American resident, let alone one with a black eye-patch. After three days of diminishing hope, I flew back to London.

'Buried him this morning, deah!' cried Muriel as I opened the door of the Colony. A letter was waiting for me:

> Not a chance of Poros for a couple of months. As half the lung was taken away, I have to learn to breathe all over again. Stairs and walking impossible. It is infuriating to be so alert and on the ball yet so physically helpless. No plane would take me – but bookings are being arranged (as soon as I can teeter up a gangplank) for me to go night sleeper to Paris where it is booked on to the Orient Express for Venice then to glide down the Adriatic in a white steamer to Piraeus where Black Patch is spending the entire summer.

When he left hospital he was driven to the Ship Hotel in Brighton where Francis had arranged for his convalescence. Smartly dressed, playing the self-made man who has 'just come down from north', Deakin toured some pubs and clubs with an old friend he met that evening. At lunchtime the next day he became short of breath and returned to his bedroom where he rang down for some tea. He was dead when they brought it.

When he filled in the usual forms in the Westminster Hospital, he had named Francis as 'next of kin'. When we met, Francis said:

> It was the last dirty trick he played on me. You know how it is, I really can't stand all those formalities. Well, they told me I needn't be next of kin at all, the state could look after him instead. I knew just what that meant – a pauper's funeral – and everyone in Soho would say I'm the meanest man in London. To my surprise that wasn't the case; the coroner assured me that Mr Deakin's bank manager confirmed there were more than sufficient funds to give the old thing a good send-off.

'Bank manager?' I asked, mystified, remembering Deakin's protests of poverty. 'You mean he had some money all the time?'

'So it would seem,' said Francis carefully. 'In fact I did give him the proceeds of one of the pictures. Seems such a waste now all of that goes to the state. Well, there it is.'

For a moment he looked dejected and then we started to laugh.

Sure enough, the Treasury solicitor inserted a notice in *The Times* (June 1973) that John Deakin had left a sum of several thousand pounds; fortunately, a brother came forward to claim it.

Meanwhile, Francis, as the 'next of kin', had the unenviable duty of identifying the body.

' "Is that Mr Deakin?" they asked.

'They lifted up the sheet and there he was, his trap shut for the first time in his life.

'It most certainly is.'

Colin MacInnes – 'He Makes Us Feel So Black'

There was a kinder, almost tender side to Colin to compensate for his rudeness. I saw this when he called one afternoon at Limehouse, trailed by a blond young man and the inevitable West Indian. Possibly the black man had been cowed by Bwana MacInnes into a state of silence, for he remained mute throughout. Just as well, for Colin spoke brilliantly as we sat on the balcony overlooking the Thames and gently drank the afternoon away. When they left he gave me a copy of *England, Half England*, though he scowled when I asked him to sign it which he did grudgingly – 'Dan from Colin' – but he left a script he had been working on – *The Boy in the Gallery* – for a musical which was never produced. We shared a passion for music hall, which I had revived at the Waterman's Arms on the Isle of Dogs.

Overcoming his dislike of pubs, Colin came to see me there and wrote it up in his page 'Out of the Way' in *New Society* (20 December 1962):

Most of us have fantasies we fail to blend into realities, but Mr Dan Farson has – to coin a phrase – made his dream come true . . . And not content with realising his own dream, Mr Farson has realised one of mine: which is that popular song and entertainment should evade the telly screens and radio to which they have been banished from the few surviving Theatres of Variety and reappear, as they did in their days of authenticity and glory, on a performer-to-audience basis where there is direct personal communication.

This is what I was trying to achieve, and he concluded, 'Can it really be that Mr Farson has squared an impossible circle?'

Sadly, the answer was no. I abandoned the Waterman's when I resigned from my television job and moved to Devon in 1964.

Colin's affection for the old music hall songs was reflected in this proposed musical, with a lavish scene when the tommies marched on board a liner on their way to fight the Boers, cheered by their families who crowded the quayside. The unabashed sentiment of music hall with its jingoism and flaunted patriotism might seem at odds with Colin's rebelliousness, yet this was true to his nature. He was a man of paradox. He behaved outrageously but was puritanical at heart; like many men who are cruel, he considered himself a man of honour; he was an anarchist on the side of authority; and he was a homosexual who could never come to terms with this condition happily.

Ostensibly the champion of the underdog, he behaved with appalling arrogance when he was transferred to the Field Security Section in Germany in 1944, lording it about, expecting the Germans to dance attendance on him as he travelled around interrogating suspected collaborators. I have been told that he insisted that the staff should line up outside and bow to him when he left a German restaurant.

Though he fought courageously for their rights, he could be as condescending to the black people he befriended as the worst type of English colonial bigot. Occasionally, he insisted that I accompany him to one of the coloured clubs in Soho, like the Myrtle Bank in Berwick Street where they served chicken and rice and Coca-Cola but no spirits, or the Abalabi, which was West Indian for 'high life' down Maidenhead Passage lit by dim gaslight. Once, when Colin went to the bar, a black man beside me turned and sighed: 'I like dat Colins, but oh man, he does make me feel so *black*!' Walking through Soho with Colin at night, Victor Musgrave noticed that he stopped to talk to black men – 'like an unofficial MP in his constituency'.

Yet Colin's concern was genuine and ahead of his time. He was prophetic in his alarm for the innocent West Indian immigrants arriving hopefully in large numbers to receive a bleak welcome from the grey London skies and a bleaker one from the Londoners themselves.

He expressed his dismay in *City of Spades*, published in 1957, and in the climax to *Absolute Beginners*, published in 1959, which described the Notting Hill race riots of 1958.

Colin's championship of the black cause was obsessional to a point where he became the white propagandist for the Black Power militant leader Michael X, rather than the impartial observer he should have been. Michael Hunte, a Barbadian who shared several flats with Colin though not his bizarre lifestyle, is a regular of the French and gave me an insight into Colin's preoccupation with blacks. 'He taught us the rules, showed us where the town hall was and told us what our rights were. He thought society was giving us a raw deal and he bullied us all the time to make more of ourselves. To us he was known as "the mystery man", a sort of Messiah. We weren't too sure why he wanted to help us, but we knew he cared for us as if we were lost souls.'

Yet the Messiah was so offensive to two West Indian Jehova's witnesses that they accused him of being the anti-Christ before they fled. Needless to say, the two witnesses were women.

There was something threatening in Colin's scowl and swagger, which Michael Hunte confirms: 'Make no mistake, Colin was aggressive. He lived on the danger line. When a driver cut in front of our mini-cab, Colin jumped out and slapped the man violently across the face, exclaiming, "How dare you do that to my driver?" '

'Was your mini-driver coloured?' I asked Hunte.

'But of course!' he smiled.

Colin was ruthless in his imposition on his friends. As an insomniac he lived a twilight existence victimising those who tolerated his behaviour by descending on their doorstep at 3 a.m. armed with a bottle of whisky and a West Indian. George Melly remembers the hours of abuse as if Colin were trying to test his attitudes, seeing how far he could go before the nerves snapped.

When he started to abuse someone whom the Mellys were fond of, Diana Melly could stand it no longer and ordered him out of the house.

'That's it!' cried Colin triumpantly, '*that*'s what I've been waiting to hear.' Though he regarded himself as the injured party, Colin decided to forgive the Mellys a few months later and called at their house revealing a surprising strength as he picked them up, one under each arm, making them join in the words of a music hall song, squeezing them painfully when they failed to do so. George was on his moped the last time he saw Colin, who stood angrily at the kerb, so George swung round in the hope that he would not be noticed, skidded, and fell off, bruising himself quite badly. As he strugged to his feet he saw Colin staring at him fixedly before he gave a dismissive gesture and wandered off smiling, for all the world as if he had jinxed his former friend.

Colin was so consistently broke in spite of his considerable earnings from journalism and broadcasting that George Melly suspected he was being blackmailed, an unfortunate though relevant word in this particular context. Michael Hunte denies this, believing that Colin simply gave the money away: 'When the phone went and he heard heard the pips, he'd mutter, "Here's another one in trouble." When he opened the door, he did not invite the caller in but pressed the money into his hand, enjoying the sense of conspiracy.'

Sharing Colin's midnight world must have been traumatic, but Michael Hunte was young and remembers the best of times – the way Colin left a large deposit at the nearest off-licence in case he fell out with the local landlord, and kept a constant supply of food for the cat which proved useful when they moved into a new street

at Christmas where every shop was shut and survived on several
tins of the cat's sardines and even more bottles of whisky.

Hunte remembers Colin with affection, and this is the point. In
spite of his cantankerousness, Colin was endearing. Also, he was a
positive force: 'I owe Colin as long as I live. He taught me how to
survive in the city. Today I'm all right and things are better for
black people.'

Far from being an outsider, Colin belonged to London: to the
City of Spades and Cable Street, where he was arrested in a
gambling club on a drugs charge, and later acquitted; to Notting
Hill where the first race riots erupted; and to Soho with its capacity
for putting people at their ease. He approved of the way that people
lived in the streets, 'and do not merely use them – as is the custom
elsewhere in English cities – as places to get from here to there.'

Absolute Beginners is a book with considerable charm, a powerful
description of the race riots, and a touching conclusion as the
young photographer runs on to the tarmac to greet the latest
planeload of West Indians in the pouring rain. It was not
surprising that people looked forward to the film with such
excitement, though the producers proved ill-advised in shouting
their wares so loudly in advance. I went to the first preview one
Sunday afternoon in 1986 and sat there increasingly angered by
the banality. Instead of the innocence of the fifties, the young
director gave the scenes a spurious sophistication with the gloss of
those tacky plywood nightclubs in low-budget B-films of that
period, with someone blowing a trumpet. I found it as authentic as
a TV commercial for a box of chocolates or the sort of video
'promo' which gave the director his reputation.

The film presented a running teenage orgy, but if you were a
teenager in the fifties the few places to go to in Soho were
wholesome to the point of boredom with a whiffle of skiffle on a
washboard and a hiss of frothy coffee from a clean machine. At
least people wanted to go out, before television kept them in, but
teenagers mostly hung about in 'caffs' or went to the cinema. There
were no discos and when the pubs closed the night was over unless

you were a member of a club, which few young people could afford. The lack of places to go to explains the huge number of wild parties which we poured into when the pubs shut in Soho, especially those given by Eleanor and Rodrigo Moynihan in Chelsea, who created a marvellously friendly atmosphere. There might have been occasional tears and the odd fight but there was no viciousness. People were simply out to enjoy themselves.

There was one new phenomenon which belonged to the teenagers alone – the onslaught of rock-and-roll, which was virtually ignored by the film. Larry Parnes had a stable of boys to be groomed into pop-stars in a basement off Shaftesbury Avenue, where I met such wide-eyed innocents as Marty Wilde and Billy Fury who were beautifully mannered in spite of the threatening new names chosen for them by Parnes. Terry Dene, who proved unable to cope with the adulation, was also there, and Joe Brown, the nicest and most intelligent of all.

The first pop-star to become a teenage idol was Tommy Steele whom I knew slightly when he played skiffle at the Two Is in Old Compton Street. Delightfully fresh, he led the teenagers on their merry dance with numbers like 'Rock with Caveman'. The next place I saw him in was a fashionable nightclub (I think it was the Stork) where the management allowed Tommy to sit with me though not to buy a drink, treating him with barely concealed contempt. This was adult curiosity of the worst kind about a new trend, good for a giggle but without sympathy.

Colin, then middle-aged, had the wit to sympathise. In a memorable phrase he described Tommy Steele as 'every nice young girl's boy, every kid's favourite elder brother, every mother's cherished adolescent son'. There was no threat from Tommy, nor from Cliff Richard. And though Billy Fury was vaunted as 'England's answer to Elvis Presley', his was a delicate echo.

Such was the innocence which the film of *Absolute Beginners* failed to recapture.

Yet Colin is partly to blame for being ahead of his time. When he wrote that 'Today, youth has money and teenagers have power', he was forecasting a trend which did not really occur until the early sixties, noted by Philip Larkin in his famous verse:

> Sexual intercourse began
> In Nineteen Sixty-three
> (which was rather late for me) –
> Between the end of the Chatterley Ban
> And the Beatles' first LP.

The cynical sixties saw the loss of innocence and the growth of teenage power, not the fifties.

The other flagrant flaw in the interpretation of Colin's book was the scale of the riots at the end. The novel makes this all the more sinister by being *less* violent. Colin pinpointed isolated pockets of hostility with Cool complaining that the Teds were stopping black youths to ask for cigarettes: 'If you offer them, they take the whole pack, and grin. If you don't, they take a smack and run.' This is a far cry from the full-scale racial warfare which created a petrol-bomb carnage in the film's hysterical climax. It distorted the danger which Colin warned us was inevitable: 'Once you'd done some people, or group, or race a wicked injury . . . you'd come back and do it again.'

Today the prejudice has gone full circle and the blacks are cast in the role of aggressor.

'What would Colin have made of this?' I asked Michael Hunte.

'He would have been appalled but he saw the danger coming. The artist always gets it right before the politician. At least Colin would have had the satisfaction of saying "I told you so".'

Observing the fuss which surrounded the film when it was released, I thought how much Colin would have savoured the controversy, if only to appear on the chat-shows to denounce it, though perverse as always, he might well have approved.

Colin's life ended with decline and illness. Must this always be the pattern? The exceptions are too rare. He went to live in the country where he was an outsider at last and his historical novels no longer struck the same vibrant chord.

Though he had relatives, he was not close to them. Throughout his life he suffered from the break-up of his parents' marriage: in 1917 when he was three years old, his mother divorced his father for cruelty. She married an Australian engineer, George Thirkell, a year later and the family sailed for Australia where Colin grew up and recalled his upbringing in *June in Her Spring* (1952), a novel he was proud of though it was neglected at the time because it dealt so honestly with homosexuality. Meeting his true father when he was twenty, Colin reverted to his original surname and developed a lifelong hatred towards his mother, an obsession which was aggravated by her success as the bestselling novelist, Angela Thirkell, which Colin took as a personal slight.

The dislike was mutual and when his mother died, Colin found that she had cut him out of her substantial will and though his brothers generously offered to share their inheritance, Colin refused on principle. He perpetuated his grievance with a brutal obituary: 'During her lifetime my late mother caused me intense embarrassment, for there she was, an immensely successful and bad writer, and there was I, scorned for so long by the cruel world yet believing I had something to say . . . I found her death a liberation.' This is dreadfully revealing, of his self-pity and their shared sentimentality. I believe he craved his mother's affection. That was his 'Rosebud'.

There is a story, which may be apocryphal, that one day Colin saw an elderly woman hurrying for a bus, and fall. Helping her up, she turned on the platform to thank him and went inside. Colin suddenly realised who she was, but his mother no longer recognised him.

Colin discovered that he had cancer at the beginning of 1976. With an aversion to hospitals, doctors and nurses, he determined to brave it out, but there was one doctor he trusted who persuaded him to have an operation because there was hope if they acted at once but none whatsoever if they delayed. They removed his

oesophagus at the end of January, replacing it with plastic –
'thereby making it impossible, henceforward, for me to speak ill of
this unpleasant substance'. This was one of the last good jokes he
made, in his article for *New Society* called 'Cancer Ward'.

He faced the ordeal philosophically and without illusions: 'The
shock to the metabolism is equivalent to being hit by a truck; and
whereas this didn't worry me twenty years ago, I wondered if my
older body could take it. And if there's one place I didn't want to
die, it was in a hospital and, in particular, on an operating table.'

When he regained consciousness, his first reaction was 'one of
rapture' at finding himself in the world again. Then a terrible
bitterness set in when he was refused the pain-killing injections of
morphia and the tablets he had been led to expect. Writing with
anger at this betrayal he explained:

> England is, after all, the land where children are beaten, wives and
> babies bashed, football hooligans crunch, and Miss Whip and Miss
> Lash ply their trade as nowhere else in the western world. Despite our
> belief [that] we are a 'gentle' people, we have in reality a cruel and
> callous streak in our sweet natures, reinforced by a decadent puritan
> strain which makes some of us believe that suffering, whether useful or
> not, is a fit scourge to the wanton soul.

He prefaced this by asking if the policy of withholding pain-
killing drugs was based on strictly medical considerations: 'I don't
believe so for a moment.'

Certainly the treatment he received sounds unnecessarily cruel,
but Colin had the added bitterness of knowing that the operation
had not cured him after all. Instead of finding a single clump of
fungus inside him, the doctors had revealed a spread of cancer in
small patches. Yet, at the very least, he managed to leave the
hospital and even make short visits abroad to Paris and
Amsterdam before he returned to Hythe in Kent, where he
continued to write until he died from a massive haemorrhage on
the evening of 23 April at the age of sixty-one. The splendid, final
diatribe in *New Society* was published posthumously.

His funeral had a suitable touch of dark comedy. He was buried at sea off Folkstone and his coffin and his friends were transported on a fishing smack which reminded Frank Norman of *The African Queen*: 'The skipper, a friend of Colin's, had bright gold rings in his ears and tattoos on his arms. A bottle of Teacher's was passed around from hand to mouth, the sun shone far too brightly and a party atmosphere prevailed.'

At the three-mile buoy, the engine stopped, the curate read the service, and Colin's coffin was shoved over the side. Though it had no lid it was covered by a nylon cloth fastened with tacks, but instead of sinking it floated barely underneath the surface as his mourners looked down in surprise.

Characteristically, for grief is a great distorter, other friends remembered the event differently.

Fiona Green heard the buoy's bell toll and saw a seagull land on the coffin and fly off 'as if it were carrying his spirit'.

Eddie Linden threw a copy of his magazine *Aquarius* which 'landed on top of the coffin and the coffin sank . . . everyone laughed'.

The undertaker was more prosaic, explaining that the coffin floated because it had been pushed into the sea the wrong way round and a crude hole was at the highest end. But it was not long before Colin disappeared.

Tony Gould noticed that there was one vital factor missing: his family was represented by his younger half-brother, Lancelot Thirkell, but no black was present.

This was fitting.

'You're on your own now,' he told Michael Hunte some years before. 'Fellows, there's not much more that I can do for you.'

So many deaths and suicides – the casualty rate was high in Soho, as if such bright spirits need to burn themselves out. Was it all worthwhile? Was the effort worth the dark brown taste, the headache and the guilt on the morning after? Was it worth the sacrifice of talent, and the shocking sums of money poured down our throats into our protesting stomachs? Was it worth the waste of time?

Oh yes! We had fun! Everything was positive, not waste at all. Compared to today's world-weary pessimism, it was a time of innocence and hope. Anything could happen, and, for some of us it did.

PART THREE
RESURGENCE FOR SOHO

The Swinging Sixties and, even more, the Cynical Seventies came close to destroying the spirit of Soho. Paradoxically, permissiveness made Soho furtive.

The worst consequence was the sprouting of sex shops, selling identical goods to the same nondescript and rather gloomy men. Instead of being erotic, the effect of these places was deeply depressing with the realisation that even the permissive society desperately needed further sexual arousal. Evidently, the carbon-copy shops met a genuine demand and the owners made a fortune in the process, sometimes an alleged £10,000 a week, and the temptation to make such money must have been irresistible when the law allowed you to get away with it and no one particularly cared.

The offence lay not with the pornography but with the plethora of shops which sold it, ousting many of the old-established stores which gave Soho its character. This was a tragedy, for you knew that when the dilator and the dildo replaced the garlic sausage, the former store had gone for good and would not return. In one case a spacious public house made way for sexy underwear; in another, an exemplary Italian grocer's became a sleazy porn shop selling 'dirty' books and magazines, though 'dreary' would be an apter description. Just as irrevocable are the so-called 'amusement arcades' and the type of shop which replaced Bifulco's Stores, the excellent butcher, in order to sell T-shirts emblazoned with the images of Ronnie and Reggie Kray.

Thea Porter, a regular at the Colony Room, closed her fashion house in Greek Street after twenty years claiming that her customers came to hate the place. 'They hesitate even to cross the street. We were opposite one porn shop and next to another. One of my Arab clients used to have me stand by her in the street while she waited for her Rolls to arrive. It's very sad. I adore the place.' In fairness, she was driven out by the drastic rise in rents as well, and this was another reason why a number of the older residents had to move on. Even so, she blamed her substantial debts on the permissive society and the liquidator agreed: 'The world's elegant women are not prepared to go to a place surrounded by sex shops and strip clubs and populated by pimps and prostitutes.'

By the end of the seventies there were nearly two hundred premises providing sexual titilation in various forms, apart from individual prostitutes. Porn was big business and Soho drifted into the doldrums as ordinary people started to keep away. Previously curiously indifferent, in the eighties the Westminster Council began to wake up to the danger, alerted by the vigilance of the Soho Society. 'Our opposition has nothing to do with morality,' said Dorothy Donaldson-Hudson, the vice-chairman, and one of the leading party-givers in the fifties. 'Soho has always been a slightly raffish area and we like it that way. We don't mind unobtrusive well-run clubs that cater for the sex-trade; they're not a nuisance. But we do object to the way that most of these places have changed the environment for the community – the noise, the dirt, the kind of people that they attract, the unpleasantness of being accosted.'

Yet, ironically, because there were so many people milling about at night, the crime rate was negligible compared to that in the suburbs. And to make Soho look 'nicer', a private member's bill was pushed through Parliament by Tim Sainsbury, preventing the open-window displays of dildos and torture – a convenient cosmetic which concealed the inner rot but hardly cured it.

In 1982 a law was passed enabling Westminster Council to impose licences and a hundred sex shops were closed down. The net was being drawn at last, but new loopholes were discovered leading to the most pathetic phase of all: that of the fourteen male and female peepshows. These ranged from 50p in the slot to watch a naked girl gyrating on a bed for one minute, to a £5 entrance fee to see a gay revue at the Colt in Berwick Street where 'naked, slender youths' danced alternate half-hours on a stage, stripping from jeans and T-shirts to their socks, with a further £1 for a quick touch, though not apparently a grope, as a sort of tip. Could anything be more forlorn? Then there were sixteen topless bars where waitresses served non-alcoholic drinks at £15 a glass and hostesses demanded fake champagne for prices up to £70 a bottle. Half-hearted touts inveigled tourists into such places and the suckers went inside in expectation of plenty; and they were conned exactly as they had been in the clip-joints of the fifties. Nothing had changed except the price.

With the possible exception of certain massage parlours, real sex was not for sale, just the promise of sex, and unlike Copenhagen it was a promise that was unfulfilled. The vice was fantasy, an illusion which offended because the reality was so bleak.

Acting decisively in 1981, Westminster Council moved in with new powers and cleaned up the district virtually overnight, allowing only 6 out of 21 applications for licences for sex shops, while the GLC renewed only 3 out of 80 applications for Soho's sex shops and cinemas.

Those who had run their shops discreetly were rewarded, like Janus owned by William O'Connor (also known as 'Bookshop Billy'), a smiling, personable young man whose company specialises in spanking and runs an international magazine for those who practise it. A local resident, the late Frankie Blake, appeared as a witness on his behalf testifying: 'Spanking, yes, but no blood drawn,' referring to the principle rather than the practice at the premises in Old Compton Street, which he described as possessing 'dignity and decorum'.

Following this positive legislation, there has been a new resurgence in the life of Soho.

The revival has been welcomed by Soho's leading personalities. Norman Balon, who runs the Coach and Horses in Greek Street, says: 'Since Westminster Council has started to clean Soho up sexually it has returned to the pleasant place to go to that it was years ago. A young man can take his lady out to dinner and then go to a pub, many of which have not been modernised but are still traditional. The original Bohemian flavour of Soho has come back. I find it's improving all the time.'

His optimism is echoed by Elena, the famous manageress who came to L'Escargot from Bianchi's when it closed. She remembers the friendliness of Soho in the fifties before it became 'sordid' with sex shops: 'Now that these are less exposed, people can walk around and not feel uncomfortable.' She notices the new spending power: 'In the old days, young people came with their parents; now it's the other way round. For many of the customers, eating out is a new experience and sometimes I have to guide them through the menu.'

It is not in the nature of Soho to be static, but in spite of the pressures the district remains remarkably unchanged. Carnaby Street near Oxford Circus catered for the 'kids' described by Colin MacInnes who had 'loot to spend at last', but the tacky attempt at trendy glamour provided a useful warning of what Soho might become if the traffic was banned to make it into a 'pedestrian precinct' (the words are ugly in themselves) with coloured bollards and quaint visual reminders of the various nationalities who settled here. Fortunately, the Soho Society is resisting plans to turn Soho into another Covent Garden.

There were moments of sophistication in the sixties, with the trattorias started by Franco and Mario; the Establishment Club in Greek Street; and the Ad Lib with fur-lined walls and tanks of piranha fish – but it is in the mid-eighties that Soho has witnessed a new vitality.

A few of the old places have gone, such as Benoit Bulcke and King Bomba, but the marvellous Lina Stores in Brewer Street continues to flourish, with fresh ravioli, bags of risotto rice, and olives stuffed with herbs and garlic, while Roma Galer still presides over the cash counter at Randall & Aubin next door.

A few stay much the same, like The French House, as it is called officially today, where Gaston has resisted all the blandishments of fruit machines, jukebox and formica, and has kept that sacred bar much as it was thirty years ago. At seventy, he is Soho's longest-serving landlord and remains the perfect host: 'Retire? Good Lord, what on earth would I do?'

Some restaurants have changed for the worse: notably Wheeler's which has been taken over by a chain called Kennedy Brookes, who failed to appreciate the joyful atmosphere created by Bernard Walsh and have changed the staff so that few welcoming faces remain, even lowering the standards of the food. It is no longer a place which makes one happy. Now Kennedy Brookes have revamped the Branganza in Frith Street with bizarre gimmicks which ignore the essential qualities needed for a good restaurant; although to be fair it is excellent for breakfast, with the bonus of being able to sit outside near the pavement in the open air. These are honourably upheld by such veterans as La Capannina in Romilly Street, a perfect example of a small but highly professional trattoria where the Italian food is first-rate and the staff friendly and efficient.

Above all, there is Victor Sassie to welcome one at the Gay Hussar at 2 Greek Street, my favourite restaurant in Soho.

Victor Sassie

Surprisingly, in view of the Hungarian food for which he is famous, Victor Sassie was born in Barrow-in-Furness. His father was a ship's joiner who supported his wife and ten children on fifteen shillings a week when he went on the dole, so Victor joined the British Hotel and Restaurant Association which sent him to

Budapest when he was seventeen where he was apprenticed to the
master restaurateur, Karoly Gundel:

> An excellent man who gave cooks and waiters status. We have no
> status in this country, no classification, we're just domestic servants,
> nothing. The British establishment thinks that catering is for
> foreigners, which explains their begrudging attitude to tourists –the
> fear of becoming a nation of hosts. Yet catering is a booming industry
> and tourism will be a major contribution if we manage to save our
> economy and not sink lower than Bulgaria.

Returning to England, he opened the Budapest in Dean Street with
himself, a chef, a waiter, and a washer-up, sometimes Jeff Bernard or
Frank Norman. A faded menu for New Year's Eve in 1940 included
Gundel Tokany named after his mentor, and goulash at 1*s*. 9*d*. The Gay
Hussar was opened in 1953 and to many it has the best atmosphere,
though the room is small, and offers the best value for the set lunch.
The one cause for complaint is Victor's benevolent tyranny as he tells
you what to eat – 'I would prefer you to have something lighter' –
brushing aside your protest that you had been looking forward to
stuffed cabbage or Debreceni sausages.

His customers gave him a surprise lunch on his seventieth
birthday in 1985 to thank him for the pleasure he has given. Deeply
fond of Soho, he says, 'I am trying to maintain the tradition of good
food at competitive prices.'

I asked Peter, his young Hungarian headwaiter, what Victor's
particular qualities are in this all-consuming profession: 'He has
two dozen,' he began, rattling off a startling list.

> He is police commissar; psychiatrist; a master chef; master salesman
> which includes master liar; master schmooze; politician; negotiator;
> spy. Always a lot of tolerance of silly people and, above all, he loves the
> trade, for you have to give up everything – your holidays, your dreams,
> your hobbies, your sex life, your family. There is nothing left except the
> work. That's why so few stick it. You have to be crazy about it,
> otherwise restaurateurs retire after fifteen years, worn out.

But this has been Victor's life since he was twenty – half a century!
Victor is the great exception!

The Soho tradition of a wide choice of restaurants has been
enhanced by a large number of newcomers, many of whom are
outstanding, like Friths; Alastair Little, and the new influx of the
excellent Korean and Thai restaurants: Bahn Thai at 21 Frith
Street, and Rasa Sayang, apart from the dozens of Chinese in Lisle
and Gerrard Streets in Soho's new Chinatown. Though northern
Soho has dwindled with scarcely a public house worth visiting
apart from the Newman's Arms, the shift south of Shaftesbury
Avenue has brought new colour and spice to the district, provided
the infiltration stops there.

With the change in the licensing laws, making it possible at last
to have a glass of wine with a civilised meal in the afternoon, there
will be a new incentive for customers and restaurateurs alike to
enjoy a privilege that other countries take for granted. In Soho, at
least, the staff should not object if properly rewarded, though I
have to admit that they did not look particularly overjoyed at the
Soho Brasserie which paved the way in 1986 when they discovered
a way of serving drinks legally until 4.30 p.m. However, the
difference in a place like Kettner's could be startling.

Kettner's is one of the great success stories of the transformation
in Soho. The old-fashioned, Edwardian restaurant, famous for the
private rooms and assignations upstairs, was taken over by Peter
Boizot when it was almost moribund, and though the restaurant
now serves hamburgers and the famous pizzas, which he started in
Soho twenty-two years ago at his Pizza Express, he has kept the
atmosphere the same, even to Alfredo the singing waiter. A piano
adds a touch of sophistication, attractive paintings decorate the
walls, and the champagne bar is so popular that it is crowded every
evening. Peter Boizot has enhanced the former style and not
destroyed it. He seems to have a Midas touch with thirty-eight
restaurants under his franchise, for he realised from the outset that
people welcome the chance to eat comparatively cheaply in

luxurious surroundings. This has been his policy for Kettner's – a triumphant blend of old and new.

The Groucho Club, where Gennaro's used to be in Dean Street, is a new type of club which has proved wholly successful. Named after the quip by Groucho Marx, that he wouldn't wish to belong to any club which would have him as a member, it was started specifically as a contemporary meeting place for the eighties, opening on 13 May 1985. Originally it was the idea of two feminist publishers, Carmen Callil and Liz Calder, who wished to cater for the independence of women, providing an antidote to the stuffy male bastion which barely tolerated members' wives. They asked Tony Mackintosh to create such a club and they joined forces: 'After all,' he points out, 'places like the Garrick won't even accept women as members. We chose Soho because it's enjoying a new lease of life.'

It strikes me as the perfect club for Soho, starting with breakfast at 9.00 a.m., continuing throughout the day with two dining-rooms, but the buzz is busiest in the early evening – though a visitor from the country might be appalled by the cost of a couple of rounds. As with Kettner's, where people pay a goodly sum for a bottle of champagne as nonchalantly as if they are ordering bitter, money is no longer a problem for the young. The 1,400 members of the Groucho are predominantly young media people – men and women.

For me, the singular success of the club is the well-designed bar which adapts to the time of day: excellent cappuccino at 9 a.m., and quiet enough to write or to read the morning papers; tea at one of the tables in the afternoon; drinks at the bar where you are bound to meet people of interest, with the lights dimmed for the early evening.

This room is instantly sympathetic and the atmosphere reflects the friendliness of the staff. The Groucho is one of the best things to happen to Soho in the eighties.

Hazlitt's is another unqualified success, a new hotel at 6 Frith Street, occupying three houses built in 1718, one of them the home of

Hazlitt himself. Restored in the old style, it is unpretentious and discreet, with the stylish simplicity of a French hotel, complete with continental breakfast and fresh croissants in the morning and your own door key, at a reasonable cost. Another enhancement for Soho.

Happily, the new Soho is expanding in many directions. 1987 saw the opening of a new art gallery, Birch and Conran, next door to the Colony, specialising in twentieth-century British art; and an excellent bookshop, in Meard Street opposite, run by William R. Barnes, devoted to rare, illustrated, twentieth-century books which are out of print. There is also a smart menswear shop next to the Golden Lion, Christopher New. Other valuable editions to Soho are Ronnie Scott's Jazz Club in Frith Street, and Dean Colour Laboratories and Gino, the Italian barber, both in Dean Street.

Pubs and Clubs for Gays

The Golden Lion has been taken over by a new management and the result is exactly what the two men intended: the pub is smarter and more respectable, verging on the twee, with signs warning customers that the 'landlord has the right to refuse anyone without having to give an explanation'.

Fortunately, while the Lion has lost its roar, the former landlords have taken over the Swiss Pub, now renamed the Compton, which had reached a low and empty ebb. Due to the initiative of Jack Fuller and Ian Hooper who brought their former bar staff with them and organised a new attraction called Special Nights, the Compton pulsates with life worthy of the Lion in its heyday. The atmosphere is less predatory but more fun, avoiding the cloistered militancy of similar pubs in the provinces.

In the sixties the Wolfenden Report helped to kill the carefree atmosphere in Soho by sweeping the tarts out of sight and allowing consenting adults to do what they liked in private. The change in the law was correct but it had a curious side-effect: once such behaviour became legal, the queers became gays and gained a new aggression, taking part in protest marches, even though there was little left to protest about – more a cause in search of a persecution. Far from breaking down boundaries, Wolfenden created a greater discrimination on *both* sides and a greater sense of isolation. In the days of the Caves everyone was too busy to bother about sexual differences and there was a marvellous mix of attitudes. What innocence there was then!

Several gay clubs have sprung up on a strictly membership or entrance-fee basis, most of them owned by Paul Raymond whose Revuebar was the first to give Soho its sexy reputation after the war. Though the splendid artist Beryl Cook is based in Plymouth, she is very much a Soho type of person and when we lunched at Langan's in March 1987 George Melly came over to tell her that she should go to Madame Jo Jo's, one of Raymond's clubs with £5 admission, bouncers outside and transvestites 'the size of cart-horses'. 'It sounds absolutely *wonderful*!' she gasped, and she told me about it afterwards.

'I loved it – it is like a theatre, and so classy. I so admired the person in the dress dancing all alone, twirling in time to the music.' She giggled: 'One thing tickled me pink: when he lay on the bar and raised his legs in time to the music and no one took a blind bit of notice – except me! We sat in the balcony and were so surprised when a man with a wig and false breasts sat down at our table, having just seen him on stage as Ruby Venezuela playing tweetie-pie in a golden cage.

' "My God," said my husband, "it's Brian."

'He was a neighbour from Plymouth. It was lovely seeing him, he does deserve to get on. Afterwards we went to the Piano Bar next door where an awfully nice man looked after us. Funnily enough he was called Beryl!'

The Survivors

Jeffrey Bernard

The Coach and Horses in Romilly Street is both an office and a second home for one of Soho's most resilient survivors, Jeffrey Bernard, who has immortalised the landlord, Norman Balon, with loving slander as an impossibly mean and outrageously difficult man. Not only has this image stuck, but Norman glories in it, to such an extent that he hands out address books to his favourite customers at Christmas which are embossed with the proud declaration 'London's rudest landlord.'

'I have created a Frankenstein monster,' says Jeff bitterly as Norman prowls around his bar like a demented Walter Matthau. Occasionally Norman feels obliged to growl like a wounded bear in order to sustain this reputation, for he is really the most genial of men. When Jeff is ill in hospital due to his diabetes, Norman is the first to visit him with such delicacies as smoked salmon, shattering the calm as he points to the surrounding patients with deafening candour: 'Look at the state of *him*! Can't be long before he snuffs it!' While Jeff cringes, Norman continues his doctor's round with gleeful insensitivity.

Back on his stool in the Coach, Jeff holds court like an exiled monarch, signing copies of his book *Low Life*, accepting the compliments of strangers and even their offers of drinks – large vodka, ice and soda. His success is delightful because it has brought him prestige which he has achieved simply by sitting on his bar stool and recounting the trials of his daily life as the vodka goes down. His column, in the *Spectator*, which has earned him a place in English journalism, has proved extraordinarily popular and I suspect that many of his readers enjoy a sense of danger vicariously before they retreat to the safety of their own suburban respectability. Its success is also due to his appreciation of the absurdities of life and the fact that he is really funny. Frank Norman should have become the Damon Runyon of Soho; Jeff has done so.

Recalling the fifties as we are apt to do, Jeff told me, 'I don't think I was ever truly happy until I started writing for the *Spectator*. There was a time when I was a builder's mate and it was absolutely awful, I was miserable.' When I suggested that John Minton would have enjoyed his success and the new vigour of Soho, he corrected me at once: 'Don't you believe it. He'd have hated our independence. He got his kicks from thrusting money on people to show that he was better. He really loathed it if you bought him a drink.'

If drinking is a form of voluntary euthenasia, Jeff is committing a protracted hara-kiri for the entertainment of his friends. I share the feeling of relief when the bolts draw back, and the only cure is the first drink of the day; miraculously it works, so the vicious circle turns again. I doubt if either of us would have it any other way. As Jeff points out, you meet a nicer class of person in the gutter or a pub. Ignorant people might say that Jeff 'has it made'. Few know the effort of making words seem effortless.

His view of Soho today is not so sentimentally rosy as mine. 'Soho was full of poets, painters, philosophers and layabouts. Of course it's gone for ever – people don't like one any more. Before, people were kinder and didn't go around beating each other up except in private criminal gangs, which was OK.'

I should point out that he makes such observations happily, vodka in hand, surrounded by new Soho friends such as Tom Baker, Michael Elphick and John Hurt, with Richard Ingrams observing the scene with amused detachment from the corner, teetotal table reserved for *Private Eye*.

Jeff is not alone in his jaundiced view. Ian Board at the Colony says that Soho is being overrun by Chinese, and Auberon Waugh, who edits the distinguished *Literary Review* from Beak Street, dislikes the smart new restaurants and wine bars – 'where young advertising men and designers can be seen living it up in an atmosphere of glossy unreality. It sounds perverted to say so but I think I preferred the old dirty-mac Soho. Given the fact that pornography is a necessary evil there is something to be said for a ghetto where a relatively blind eye is turned to the sale of dirty books and pictures.'

Bruce Bernard

It was years before I realised that Bruce's frequently glum exterior concealed a delightfully sharp sense of humour. He views his brother's success with bemusement.

'Are you Jeff's brother?' someone asked him in the Coach.

'No,' he replied with a terseness worthy of the Duke of Wellington, 'Jeff is my brother.' As he is four years older, this is correct.

When Jeff gave a party with Geraldine Norman in the Portland Street flat which they shared, a woman found herself outside Jeff's bedroom and looked inside at the walls, which were covered with photographs of Jeff posing with the rich and famous.

'Would this be Jeff's room?' she asked.

Bruce smiled. 'If not, it must be someone who likes him very much.'

Benefiting from his experience as picture editor of the *Sunday Times Magazine* and his own instinct as a painter, Bruce has struck a rewarding vein with a series of books he has written and compiled: *The Bible and its Painters* (1983) – my personal favourite; *Vincent by Himself* (1985) – combining the letters and paintings of Van Gogh – which became a bestseller here and in America; and *The Impressionist Revolution* (1986). His taste is infallible and his books encourage you to look at the artists again with fresh eyes, finding something new even in the work of such a familiar painter as Renoir.

Always the champion of Deakin's photography, Bruce put his loyalty into effect in September 1984 when he organised an exhibition of his work at the Victoria and Albert Museum: 'John Deakin – The Salvage of a Photographer'. The catalogue quoted Francis Bacon:

I am very pleased that the Victoria and Albert Museum has arranged this exhibition of John Deakin's photographs – because his work is so little known when one thinks of all the well known and famous names in photography – his portraits to me are the best since Nadar and Julia Margaret Cameron.

A book of Deakin's photography for *Vogue* is due for publication soon, compiled by Jane Ross. Belatedly, Deakin is now recognised as one of the outstanding photographers of the century.

Henrietta Moraes

Henrietta Moraes is another survivor who has won through against the odds. At one point she was imprisoned for theft and cat-burglary when she was suffering from amphetymine poisoning. 'It gave me what sailors and soldiers had in the war – it made me so bloody *brave*! I met someone on the roller-coaster at Battersea Fun Fair and my life became completely criminal but I didn't know that. All I remember is climbing up drainpipes and over roofs, that's all. It was like trying to climb the Matterhorn, it takes away your fear. It's madness.'

Later, on lysergic acid, she hallucinated completely – submerged with angels and devils. When she came out of Holloway, the Colony started a fund which raised £1,000 though as with Archer they tried to restrain her from spending it – 'but the one thing you want to do when you leave Holloway is *freak*!'

Ironically, when she broke her dependence on drugs she discovered that she was no longer dependent on Soho either – 'I had a whole lot of new people. You can have enough.'

In the fifties Henrietta thought that Francis Bacon was the most fascinating man she had seen and went to the French pub every day in the hope of meeting him, as she did. Today, strangers come up to her saying, 'You're Henrietta Moraes, aren't you, the Francis Bacon', referring to the paintings he based on her. 'To be recognised as a painting which was done thirty years ago, it's most odd, being metamorphosised into a Bacon!' She laughs at the irony, especially as Francis Bacon commissioned Deakin to photograph her naked but turned her upside down adding a hypodermic needle with three blood-spots on the sheets – 'How did he *know*!' she exclaims. 'That happened ten years later. Is he a prophet?'

After Deakin took the photographs, Henrietta happened to go to an afternoon drinking club she hardly knew where she was greeted with shouts of gleeful recognition from several sailors she had never seen before. Explaining their hilarity, they brandished the prints which Deakin had just sold them for ten shillings each showing Henrietta posing nude and on the striped mattress showing all.

'At first I was livid. Then I laughed so much, but I have not forgiven Deakin. Ten shillings indeed! He could have *given* them away!'

Ian Board

The Colony remains my favourite in Soho. Seeing a film-clip of the club in the fifties, reshown in Jeffrey Bernard's *Arena* in 1987, it was moving to see Muriel Belcher looking so happy. She was gay in the loveliest sense of that word and remained constant.

On one of my last visits to the club while she was there, I nearly collided with a man in a raincoat and inferior bowler hat who was hurrying out with a well-worn leather case. It was opening time on Saturday and the club was empty apart from Muriel and Ian.

'You know who that was?' she asked me coldly.

I shook my head nervously, with images of torn faces creeping back to me uneasily, echoes of trouble on the day before.

'*That*,' she informed me, 'was the man who was kind enough to come here on a weekend to repair the phone which you smashed yesterday.' She continued her indictment without blinking and without a pause for breath: 'Not only did you break the phone when I was expecting some important calls but you upset one of my best-spending customers who may never come here again and in all my years in club business I doubt if I have ever witnessed such disgraceful behaviour and do you know I don't give a fuck so what are you having to drink?'

I sighed with relief, knowing I was home.

When Muriel died, it was the end of many close friendships, and for Ian Board most of all; he had worked with her for years behind the bar. They met when he was a young commis waiter at the Jardin des Gourmets in Greek Street:

> One particular day she was in to lunch with Otto Lucas and others. Without sounding too corny, all I can say is that our eyes met, and everything clicked magically. At a later date Muriel said, 'I've just opened a new club. Any time you want a job, gel, you come along to me.' That was the beginning of a relationship that has combined mother, father, brother, sister, friend, partner – in fact, the lot.

Jeff and I gave the addresses at her memorial service at St Paul's Church, Covent Garden, on Thursday 29 November 1979. Deeply saddened, Francis took me to lunch at Wheeler's beforehand, where he helped me prune my addess, which was too wordy. It is hard to avoid platitudes on such occasions, but I started by saying what I felt: 'I cannot imagine a finer opportunity than a service like this to give thanks, as we do now, for our great good luck in knowing Muriel Belcher who turned life into a marvellous party.'

Fortunately, and this is the best epitaph she could have, the club continues with Ian Board who has kept the same abrasive atmosphere. There are days when I climb those dank stairs to find the place empty and depressing, but there have always been such days, and I have returned an hour later to find it bursting with vitality. At such moments it seems that little has changed.

People say that Soho is not what it used to be. 'It never was!' cries Ian.

His rudeness is legendary though no one pays much attention and the barman Michael has the patience of a saint. It is still possible to capture the atmosphere of the fifties, that nostalgic era of Soho in its heyday, especially when Francis Bacon is there.

Francis Bacon

Francis Bacon is the most astounding survivor of all. Though acknowledged as 'the greatest living painter' he remains unspoilt. His resilience is such that I have seen him looking grey after a night at Charlie Chester's gambling club in Soho, only to find him radiant in the afternoon, laughing as uproariously as ever. Always disciplined, he retains the compulsion to paint in the early hours of the morning, never losing his excitement over the latest work.

'I'm doing a triptych. One of the panels is based on the assassination of Trotsky.'

'Will there be blood?' I ask.

'Yes, there will be some blood.'

At the age of seventy-eight he has altered remarkably little. He looks years younger and poses for the camera with the slack-jowled vacancy of an idiot child, which is odd considering that he is single-minded. He remains unaffected. Honours have been offered him which he refuses with open contempt; and when his accountants advised him to live in Switzerland he laughed at such a preposterous idea: 'Can you imagine anything more boring? All those *views*!'

His mews house in South Kensington still looks as if it is waiting for the furniture to arrive, though the blankets have gone from the windows, which are now painted over in black. The light-bulbs remain as naked as ever.

Though he has appeared a few times on television since that first interview in Wheeler's, his face is scarcely public.

In one Soho pub, a man offered him a job doing up a house when he was told that Francis was a painter. At other times, someone might ask, 'How's it going, Francis?' and when he gives a shrug of mock despair, assures him: 'Don't worry. I expect it'll turn out all right.'

Conversely, during one of our last lunches at Wheeler's before it was spoilt, an American couple stopped at our table and the man apologised: 'We just wanted to tell you, sir, what an honour it is to be in the same room.' At such moments I am reminded that he receives greater respect in Italy, France and America, where one painting sold at Christie's for more than a million pounds in 1987, though the money did not go to himself.

He says, 'My mother made me promise never to grow old, and now I know what she means,' but he still seems younger than the rest of us.

A young barman at the Groucho Club, who hopes to become a full-time painter himself, asked me, 'What is he like?'

'Deeply serious,' I said. 'Humorous, tough, astounding, an original, devoid of doubt, sometimes terrible, immensely kind – *everything*.' Yet it sounded inadequate. How do you explain genius? I added: 'He says it's necessary to re-invent the language of paint, and he has done exactly that.'

Today the champagne may be a better vintage and when he took me to Annabel's the caviar was sent back so often because it was salty that we ended up with eggs and bacon. But he remains uncorrupted by the trappings of success.

In 1986 the Tate honoured him with a second retrospective: a happy occasion when he was surrounded by old friends and new, like John Edwards, the subject for several of his latest portraits.

Francis alone has made Soho worthwhile for me. There are still those days of exhilaration when the door of the Colony opens and he enters with a smile breaking across his face: 'The most extraordinary thing has just happened . . . look, do you want some champagne? Good. Well, as I was saying, and you may not believe this, but . . .'

And so I miss my train, as I have done so many times before, preferring to linger in Soho and join in the laughter.

Postscript to the Pimlico Edition

Soho and its inhabitants have of course continued to change since this book was first published in 1987. Francis Bacon, described here as 'the most astounding survivor of all' sadly died in early 1992. However, it was the sort of death that he would have wanted, avoiding all fuss, and his work lives on. Jeffrey Bernard has become a legend in his own lunchtime, due to Keith Waterhouse's play about him, *Jeffrey Bernard is Unwell*, set in the Coach and Horses. Ian Board continues to run the Colony Room which flourishes despite the pubs being open in the afternoon and which attracts a new generation of young artists. The French pub remains busy despite Gaston Berlemont's departure. And, in the face of the recession, new restaurants open as others close.

   People still say that Soho is not what it used to be. But, then, as Ian Board observed, it never was. Soho's personality has always thrived on change but its distinctive flavour magically survives.

Index

174 INDEX